A Road Less Travelled

Travelled

ANDREW SHAW

Green Cat Books

FIRST EDITION

Published in 2021 by
GREEN CAT BOOKS
19 St Christopher's Way
Pride Park
Derby
DE24 8JY

www.green-cat.shop

DEDICATION

For my dad, who sadly passed away this year
He would have loved reading this book.

And

For my mum who will probably never read it for fear of
ruining her image of me!

Thank you for suggesting that I go travelling…

I love you both.

Also, thanks to my Uncle Michael for leaving his worldly
possessions to me and enabling this epic adventure!

CONTENTS

ACKNOWLEDGEMENTS

I would like to thank my dear friend Carla for encouraging me to keep going when I got bored or frustrated with the process (especially the editing). She has been the organizational rock that allowed me to focus on the creative side and this book simply wouldn't have happened without her input and support.

Thanks to Leanne at Sheaf Design, for turning my terrible sketch into that beautiful cover and to the team at Green Cat, my publishers, for helping Carla to guide me through this process, and turning my words into this stunning work of art.

To Jez, Emma, Tom, Ayesha, Amy, Little Gav and all the other characters in this book, thank you for making 2002 the most epic of all years. Spending this time with you was life affirming and I am grateful for every moment. I hope we are all still friends after you read this book!

Disclaimer:
These stories have been told to the best of my recollection with the minimum of artistic license, although 20 years passed before I started writing, and my memory recall is not as good as it once was.
What was I saying? Oh yes. It's a pretty accurate account but some of the characters names have been changed to protect the innocent, and not so innocent.

Chapter 1 — "Shit, The Van is on Fire!"

The hostel in Townsville was a shit hole, typical city hostel, creatively advertised as exposed brickwork (concrete blocks), industrial design (rusty bed frames), vibrant colourful artwork (puke green wall with rusty watermarks and rising damp), and the '120 thread Egyptian cotton' bedding, maybe that was the number of visible stains, who knows.

'Bruce's Backpackers' was situated on the ninth floor of a nondescript corner building, a few blocks from 'downtown', otherwise occupied by offices and a ubiquitous 7-Eleven on the corner. It was early Sunday morning, and the windowless reception was eerily quiet. We were glad to be leaving.

As most of the hostel slept, as the 'Secret Seven' of us stepped into the rickety lift. Despite my bleary eyes, my gaze was drawn to a sign, 'Max 12 PAX'.- I was glad there was only seven of us. It was tiny, and in my hungover state I shuddered at the thought of another five people joining us. I was feeling a little claustrophobic.

I allowed my thoughts to drift, mainly in an attempt to take my mind off the sticky sweat forming on my brow, *"What the hell does PAX even mean anyway?"* I mused. Suddenly the lift shook me awake. It thundered so quickly downwards, the red floor indicator could barely keep up and before we knew it, it slammed to a halt.

The red floor light followed; 3….2….1….

Why had we stopped on L1? My heart raced, something felt wrong. Were we trapped between floors or was the lift about to plummet to the ground and squash us all from the feet up? I briefly wondered if jumping at the moment of impact really could save you from a lift crash – I doubted it, and in any case my reactions would have been severely slowed by the 'goon' of cheap sweet white wine that had been consumed not too many hours ago.

Then I remembered the Aussies use 'L1' to denote the ground floor and not 'G'. Clearly thumbing their nose to the stupid Poms and our colonial ways – maybe this was some ruse to try and take the land back from the English, start a republic and establish a master race of surf dudes and girls called Sheila.

The seven of us stepped out into a side alley; even though it was just gone 7 a.m., the bright sun blinded us as we stumbled over a pile of split bin liners overflowing from a huge, dirty yellow dumpster. The stench was vile; Tom retched.

"Pussy," someone snorted as we all hoisted our packs and marched off, narrowly avoiding the piles of rotten food and what looked like human waste in the alley.

It was already 30 degrees in Northern Queensland as we tiptoed carefully toward the car park in our flip flops. I almost added to the detritus as I imagined the squelch between my toes that would have followed one slight misstep. I regained my composure as Bertha came into view.

Backpacking is a way of life, a culture, an identity. The minute you put on a backpack you change fundamentally as a person, you will never ever be the same again. It's truly transformational.

The normal rules of 'cool' go out of the window, and even the more practical-minded of us lose our shit totally. Being a backpacker is like one long acid trip – all your previous realities disappear, and the world looks like rainbows and unicorns. No one gives a shit what they look like, and even non-Americans use the word 'dude'.

Backpacking comes with its own uniform and unwritten rules which every backpacker knows. The uniform is flip flops, Boardies and a wife beater. Pussies can add a hat (or worse, sunglasses), and as for sunscreen, there's nothing cool about 'slip-slap-slop' as a slogan so fuck that – backpackers are way too cool!

Let me just take a moment out here to talk about the 'uniform':

FLIP FLOPS:

Personally - I find flip flops are uncomfortable in hot weather, they rub like hell and God forbid they get wet, you will be slipping around like Bambi on ice. But worse, they break – almost as frequently as your nan breaks wind. That didn't stop me buying a pair or three.

Just like your nan's flatulence, a broken flip flop is always unwelcome but never a surprise. When one breaks, you end up walking along the street faced with the choice…. one bare foot or two?

You don't want to look like a total prick, hobbling along with one flip flop, (actually, now it's just a flip or a flop, but not both), so probably best to take the other one off too. Right? No matter the debris, broken glass, hypes or condoms you might stand on – no one wants to be just a flop.

The poor flip flop is degraded further by our hosts. The Aussies actually don't call them, flip flops, they call them 'thongs'. You probably know a thong to be a very small slip of underwear, mostly worn by women, at the behest of men (contra to any thoughts of comfort), in an attempt to be 'sexy'.

Whether it's a bit of cheese wire between your toes or your bum cheeks, it's just never going to be comfy. Every real backpacker ever has a tale of flip-flop woes, but they remain standard uniform.

WIFE BEATER:

A wife beater is a T-shirt with no sleeves; a vest, a singlet, a basketball-style jersey. Backpackers usually wear one adorned with a beer logo, which is probably hugging a bit too tight to the newly-formed 'traveller's belly'. I often wonder where my six-pack went!

The term 'wife beater' assumedly comes from the propensity for domestic abuse among the 'regular' members of society who adorn themselves in such attire. Frankly, I wouldn't be seen dead in one at home, and I certainly wouldn't wear one to beat up my wife.

I told you backpacking changes you!

BOARDIES:

Boardies are shorts made for surfing that show at least two inches of your butt crack.

They usually have only one pocket which is just big enough to fit a $10 note in, which is fine, as the money in Australia is all plastic so getting your dosh wet is not like when you put your 501s in the wash and the money left over from the bar last night has been turned into a sweaty Betty*.

Some fancy Boardies have a second pocket, which contains a nit comb and a bit of elastic. Apparently, it's a wax comb to even out the wax distribution on your surfboard - WTF? Yeah, blew my mind too. No backpacker I knew got good enough at surfing to ever need that shit.

So, totally impractically-attired we set off north. I was feeling rough from the box of wine (fondly known as a 'goon') from the night before, so I asked Tom if he wanted to drive. He was keen.

The van trip had started in Melbourne when Little Gav and I bought the VW, well, I bought it, Gav came along, but as always he had not got any cash, we'd only left England a month or so earlier. Bertha was mine!

A Sweaty Betty is a piece of paper, often a bus ticket or piece of jotter, stuffed into a student's mouth chewed, surreptitiously at the back of class, into a ball of papier macher and then thrown onto the ceiling where it would (hopefully) stick, dry out and remain for years.

I had met Tom at a much nicer hostel in Melbourne shortly after (Gav and) I bought the van, which he never really got to use as he had long since returned to Blighty – but that's another story.

Tom and I had been bumping into each other for the last six months, all the way up the east coast but this was the first time he had been in Bertha (certainly anything as old as Bertha, and possibly anything with a female name).

Tom was eccentric but then he's from Swindon, so that explains a lot. About the same age as me but somehow seemed a lot older. I had two years' work experience and three years at uni behind me. All I really knew about Tom was that he liked tennis and little kids. No, not like that – he's not Rolf Harris - he enjoyed teaching them tennis, as far as I could tell, at summer camps which ran all year round in the US.

We bonded over our shared hatred for Paul Collingwood, successful England cricketer, later to be awarded an OBE, as Shane Warne once put it "for scoring 23 not out". He couldn't bat or bowl. Tom, we were right, talentless people can make it… Look, I even published a book!

Bertha was a 1980 faded (obviously it had been in the ozone-less glare of the sun for 20 years) yellow VW camper with a white roof. The surfboards me and Little Gav had bought in Bali and had carried all around Australia, but never really even stood up on (except on the beach), were lashed to the top by a deeply frayed bungee cord that looked as old as the van.

It was hardly a pussy magnet, but Amy and Ayesha were keen to ride along rather than go on the OZ-BUS that the other two friends were about to catch. My mind drifted... Ahh Ayesha... a cross between an Amazonian princess, Indian Goddess and a page three girl... Perfect.

It was certainly not going to be a sex fest, drawing lots to see who would get to romp around in the back of the van and who would have to risk rolling around with an Eastern Brown in the bush...We had a fifth member of the tribe: Jez. (Also, Ayesha and Amy were probably too classy for that type of shenanigans.)

Jez is the nicest man you will ever meet, and even though we had known each other a few short weeks, he did something for me, for which I will always owe him a lifetime of gratitude. On Magnetic Island, a few days prior, he really took one for the team – big style. But back to the road trip.

After several weeks on Magnetic Island and sailing on the Whit Sundays, we were back on the road, heading north.

Next stop Cairns.

We quickly left behind the industrial backdrop of Townsville and picked up Highway 1. The four lane 'motorway' slowly gave way to one lane on each side with no central barrier. It was a great road surface, which is just as well as it's the only main trunk that serves the northern tip of Queensland, home to the Great Barrier Reef.

The buildings became more and more sparse, and after a

short while all we could see was bush (make your own jokes here), the natural beauty of Australia's countryside, interspersed with farms packed with millions of sheep. It really was beautiful.

The minidisc player, attached to the cassette player by some funky mechanism, boomed out Shakira (Shakira, Shakira, you know the one!). We rolled the windows down. It was hard work winding the manual handles and the hot air blew in and didn't cool us down, but we didn't care. Life was just about perfect.

We chugged along at about 90 clicks per hour and weren't holding too many people up. The ones in a rush whizzed past us up the hills as Bertha wheezed and spluttered. The thoughtful Aussie Highways Commission put in a second lane on the steep hills, so people could overtake shitty vans like ours!

About 90 minutes in, hangovers now clear, we were happily singing along to the music in the front, while Jez was trying to get a threesome going in the back. The fluffy purple bench seat was not quite big enough for the three of them and he was seemingly wedged in between these nubile young ladies.

As I looked around, he flashed a smile resembling Peter Stringfellow. But before 'Stringfellow' even had time to wink back, Ayesha clipped him behind the ear and he was told, in no uncertain terms that for the rest of the journey he would be on the floor. I knew from that moment on that Ayesha was 'in love' with me!

He perched on his backpack like a naughty schoolboy, no doubt contemplating the rationale of coming in the van when he could have been on the Oz bus he had already paid for. Only five hours to go. Chin up…dude!

My smugness was snapped as Tom dug me in the ribs.

"Hey – dude – we are losing power," he said.

"It's probably just the steep hill," I retorted, affronted that he was criticising my Bertha and that he had pulled me out of my Ayeshan daydream. We crested the hill and the road flattened out, and Tom once again piped up

"The power dude – we have no fucking power – my foot is flat to the floor."

"Pull her over, let's take a look," I urged. As I said this, I glanced in the wing mirror to make sure that we weren't about to get squashed by a 50 ton semi-trailer, but all I could see was FLAMES.

"Shit – the van is on fire!"

Chapter 2 — Don't Go Backpacking with Just Anyone

It was 2001 and I had very fortunately graduated from Loughborough University with a degree in Chemistry.

I have no idea how I managed to achieve my 2nd Class Honours degree (lower 2nd at that!) … actually, that's a lie, I do know how and if you permit me, I will share it with you. There's more than one way to get an education.

I spent three years playing sport, drinking 99p pints of Purple Nasty (snakebite and black) eating post-nightclub curries and chasing the 'ladies', which was harder than it may sound at Loughborough, as the ratio was rumoured to be one girl to every eight guys at the uni. How did I miss that in the prospectus? Schoolboy error – quite literally.

As a dual colour sportsman (cricket and football) I had been offered an easy passage into the chemistry faculty, who it seems, were more than keen to have a sportsman and a "scholar" in their midst. With an unconditional offer at A-level, I tossed off the last six months at school, hit the gym (to beef up for the ladies), spent a lot of time playing and watching cricket, and generally bumming around and delivering Chinese take-outs whilst listening to Oasis. I felt like Liam Gallagher.

Three years later, I was barely doing enough to get by. I was summoned back to the university after the end of my final exams to attend a 'viva' - an 'independently' administered oral examination to determine whether I would get a Thora or a Desmond. Everyone loves an oral exam – I smiled briefly at my own joke – the fear of re-sitting a year wiping away the smut that pervaded my 21-year-old mind.

A "Thora (Hird)" or less colloquially known, a Third-Class degree, would further embarrass the faculty that their blue-eyed boy had not only managed to play 2nd XI Cricket and 3rd XI football but had also flunked his studies. The Administrations Director surely would be fired.

All my 'hard work' was rewarded however, and the department's blushes were saved when I was able to ace the viva. The independent invigilator was amazed, the Head of Faculty was bemused, and I basked in the glory of getting the Desmond. (Desmond Tutu = 2:2 = Lower Second-Class). It was the 90s and middle-class rhyming slang was in vogue – but then again, so were the Spice Girls.

How did I do this you may ask... I had managed to 'befriend' the only girl on my course and had 'entertained' her well enough over the three years and she had occasionally helped me with work (I copied her lab reports) otherwise I may not have even got this far. Fortunately for me, she also needed a viva, but hers was to determine whether she'd get a Geoff (Geoff Hurst = First-Class Honours) or not, so she was much more advanced as a chemist than I.

She was a natural, both as a chemist and at her body hair management. She came out of the 'Invigilation Room' -

just the name filled me with dread – after her Oral Examination by two septuagenarian males – eek.

I was next but one to go in. She flashed me a smile and sat down next to me, bringing me back from a very dark place. Apart from in the lab, I had never been this close to her when sober but was too polite to say anything (or maybe too scared as she could have beaten me up – no doubt). I hope she doesn't read this book!

Unprompted, she began to tell me everything they had asked her in her viva. She explained it was so obvious that the covalent bond of an oxymoron didn't really exist and two hydroxy atoms must shift to the left with a Macarena and the MDMA would form like magic. I nodded and actually listened – in the vague hope I may learn something or at least not to get beaten up.

What seemed like an eternity later, my name was called, and I said goodbye, never to see her again.

I entered the room and they asked me the exact same questions they asked her. What luck! My old granny used to say "Andrew, there's no such thing as luck". Job done, smug smile, Desmond for me!

Lucky bastard, I said to myself probably a million times, as I powered up the motorway fresh with the realisation that I would never have to study again in my lifetime.

Degree 'earned'… Learning done. Beer…

The next two years passed without incident. Well, my heart was broken by a woman who I believe is now working for MI6, I got a job, became a development scientist (I still have the business card), doubled my salary after six months and left 'science' behind. I was now Operations Manager. Outside of work I played cricket, retired from football, drank far too many triple vodkas and fake Red Bulls at the Court House Pub with Little Gav and generally bumbled through life.

Then my uncle died. 43. Cancer.

I'd like to say, with my mortality realised, a flash bomb went off in my head telling me to travel; seek enlightenment, spirituality and cultural experience, but that would be a lie.

I had received enough inheritance to buy a lovely little house about 15 minutes from my parents, which would mean I could walk home from my cricket club – I would have even more time for vodka, perfect.

Just before I put an offer in on the cottage, my mum said we needed to have a chat. I thought she was going to talk me out of moving "so far away" from home when she said, "Son, your dad and I wondered if you had thought about travelling."

So much for my school-teacher parents not wanting me 15 minutes away, they wanted me to leave the country. My 2:2 was respectable and had long since diminished the ignominy of my almost total flop at A-level. I had a good job, was captain of my cricket club and was just about to own my home outright. The stuff of dreams (I'd say the American dream, but I am not American, and I think their dream is stupid!).

That one sentence changed my mindset and changed my life.

This book is about the outrageous escapades of a lower middle-class boy (working-class if you ask my parents), gifted but always looking for the short cut, who thought he knew it all but had semi-successfully blagged his way through life so far.

So, I set off to find myself. Prompted towards enlightenment, culture, mind-broadening experiences and spirituality; that wasn't quite how it worked out.

The spirituality I realised was mainly top shelf. The mind-broadening experiences were more mind bending, and although I did experience many local cultures it was far from enlightening for me and surely worse for them!

I basically flash-packed my way around the world like some kind of hedonistic ancient Greek warrior, without the rape and pillaging, and I didn't sack any cities, but it was a time of total abandonment of societal norms and expectations, the most fun time of my entire life. My very own form of spiritual awakening.

I was about to learn more about life in the next 12 months than in the previous 22 years. Let the 'learning' begin....

Chapter 3 — From Barnsley to Bangkok

So, at the end of October 2001, I had handed in my resignation and I was planning the trip of a lifetime.

I spent hours on the computer, researching, not because I am diligent but because it was 2001, I had 56k dial up* internet.   If you don't know what that is, get an encyclopaedia from the library and look it up... but what you need to know is, it was fucking slow.   It took three days to download a movie back then – seriously.

I read a sanctimonious 'Myspace blog about 'How to Backpack', then I browsed – slowly – wondering why I needed to leave my music behind to truly find myself. The STA Travel website suddenly loaded, and I saw round-the-world tickets advertised at less than £900...for six stops. Research done, I did what no one would think of doing now - I went to the shop to book it.

I was just getting into the car when my next-door neighbour, Little Gav, said, "Ey up, where you off to?"

Glibly, I responded, "Around the world."

Unfazed and in all seriousness, he retorted, "Can I come?"

I shrugged and said, "Sure."

That was it - decision made. We got in the car, went to Meadowhall and booked two six-stops-round-the-world tickets.

*Slower than H+ on your phone.

Oh, and I spent over £500 on one of those new-fangled digital cameras which I had previously thought were only used by paedophiles. Apparently not. It was massive and heavy with lots of wires and extras, but I was so proud of the five megapixels of quality it gave me.

We spent the next few weeks talking about how many birds we thought we could pull, which clubs to go to and analysing which four destinations we wanted to go to, other than New Zealand and Australia. I had no clue what was after New Zealand – when I say after, I mean east. The rule of the ticket was eastern flight only – truly around the world.

Thailand – Bali – Australia – New Zealand – Fiji – Canada was the eventual trip we decided on.

The first two were deemed the safest in Southeast Asia and had the best parties. Fiji was deemed a good place to break the 10,000-mile flight to North America. I discounted the USA, as I had been societally conditioned to hate the Yanks, so Canada it was!

In December 2001, with Little Gav's mum strangely bawling her eyes out – she ruled their house with an iron fist and up to this point I had thought she was too cold for tears – we stepped onto the National Express coach from Barnsley, bound for Bangkok. To be clear, the coach was going to London – a plane would take us to Bangkok.

During the five-hour drive, it hit me that Little Gav's mum's tears may have been caused by abject fear – 12 months later, I knew I was right!

Chapter 4 — It's Not as Hot as They Said It Would Be

We arrived in Bangkok and as we walked from the plane to collect our bags, I commented, "Hey, mate, it's not as warm as they all reckon."

"Yeah," he replied, "I guess not. Do you reckon we can smoke a bifter soon?"

I almost shat myself. "What, you smuggled weed into Thailand – are you fucking mental?!"

"Nah, chill, Shawzy," he snorted as though it were a crazy suggestion, which it might have been if he hadn't sneaked a block of skunk on the plane to Turkey, in his wallet, a year or two before.*

I barely got my breath back before we left the airport. I had booked a hotel for the first three nights while we acclimated, but I had not thought about the trip from the airport to the hotel. We stepped through the automatic doors to be met by a wave of heat – like opening up the oven.

"Warm enough for you, Shawzy?" Gav chuckled. I had never been in an airport that needed air-con before!

As naïve as we were, we realised that we looked like

*On that trip you could still smoke on some planes – can you imagine the pilot coming on the PA these days and advising passengers "If you'd like to smoke, please use the back five rows"? He rolled a joint and no-one seemed to care – 1999, what a great year!

stupid tourists and if we stood around with dumb looks on our faces, we might get robbed or shot. In our infinite wisdom, we hopped on a local bus. Local buses in Thailand have no air-con – it would be useless as they have no windows, save for a few wooden slats to stop you falling out.

Gav looked at me and said, "This hot enough for ya?!"

"Fuck off – you already said that!" I snorted.

It was 32 degrees and 100% humidity. We squashed in – three people on the tiny bench seat, backpacks on our laps, the only English speakers on the bus. I frantically thumbed through the Lonely Planet (remember them?!) to see where the hotel was. I couldn't find the area, so we did the next best thing and alighted on the Koh San Road.*

We looked around for a few minutes and got in a cab! We spent 45 minutes covering possibly one mile, thankfully in air-conditioned luxury. We saw two crashes, and our taxi had its wing mirror pretty much taken off by a passing tuk-tuk. I shouted angrily after the culprit aghast, but to no avail. The driver stoically wound down the window and pulled the now smashed mirror back into place. As he did so the heat rushed in… I glanced over at Little Gav (LG), he started to speak but I cut him off.

"If you mention that it's hot once more while we are here, I will punch your fucking lights out!" We laughed so loud… it was almost time for a beer.

*Made famous by the beach.

Chapter 5 — Ripped Off in Bangkok

I always say you have never really been to a country until you have been ripped off.   Sometimes it's funny, sometimes totally fucking infuriating.

We arrived at the poshest hotel ever to be stayed in by backpackers. I had splashed out; partly to try and show LG's mum I was a responsible friend who could be trusted with her son, but partly 'cos I was secretly not looking forward to 16-bed dorm rooms for the next year. For the princely sum of £35 we had a suite of two queen-sized beds, a sofa, mini-bar and typical Thai adornments.   It wasn't just posh for backpackers, it was posh for two lads from Yorkshire. (Mum, we are definitely middle-class!).

Some 24 hours after we left Barnsley, we were ready for Bangkok. We had been told 'on good authority' that there was an excellent music festival not that far away and given the address by the 'bell-boy', the last one I would see for a year.

He called us a cab and said, "Have a good night – krup."

We waved our thanks and got in the taxi, handing the hand-written note to the driver.

"Ok – krup," were his only words – he nodded, we were off.

I had clocked this guy, as the 'wise traveller' I was, I leaned forward and pointed to the meter. After some unrecognisable utterings he extended a digit and with a beep the meter came on. Smugly I sat back and explained to LG that it was best to have the meter on, save fighting about an inflated fare later on. He nodded – nonplussed. I was happy.

We hit some more traffic, but that's Bangkok. It was only light and within 20 minutes we arrived, and I duly paid the 300 THB fare, which was £6. I tipped him another 50 THB (I wasn't a proper backpacker yet). I saw a quizzical look on Little Gav's face as we stood at the entrance to the music festival.

Self-righteously reading his mind, I filled the quiet, announcing, "See, it was only £6, he could have tried to charge us £10 or even £20 if we hadn't had the meter on."

Gav didn't reply, rather he lifted his right arm, pointing directly across the street.

I looked to my right and saw it just as he spoke, "Isn't that our hotel?!"

We entered the 'Music Festival', an outdoor venue, and we took one of the plastic tables near the back, among probably 500 Thais. We didn't care we were the only Westerners there, as we enjoyed a few beers and listened to a couple of decent Thai groups play. They weren't bad and some songs were even in English.

When the bands stopped, the karaoke started; we took that as our cue to leave. We walked the 150 yards back to the hotel!

Chapter 6 — "The Cambodian Princess" and Near-Death Experience 1/3

"Let's go to that place the bus dropped us off at yesterday," Gav said as I poured through the Lonely Planet to find somewhere to have a night out and not get ripped off again.

"Cool – let's do it," I agreed, tossed the LP on the bed and headed for the door. After a tame start the night before we were up for a proper night out.

We eased ourselves in with a Bintang* or two in a pool hall style bar. Pool was played in pairs, and it was winner stays on. If you managed to win 20 games in a row, you won a big cash prize and a big bottle of Belvedere (or maybe Sang Som!).

We played pool with and beat some of the sexiest women on the planet. We also eased past some other backpacker pairs. We were on fire.

After remaining unbeaten for about an hour Gav announced, "That one fancies me, I am going to chat her up."

This was strange as she was likely to speak little or no English. It was more strange, as Gav had never chatted a bird up in his life. We carried on playing and between shots he went off to make small talk with the small Thai girl with the small top and very small shorts.

Local Beer.

A Kiwi lad who we had played pool against a few frames before came over to me.

"Alright, I am John. You and yer mate are good players."

"Thanks. Andy," I replied, holding out my hand by way of introduction. We chatted and laughed at Gav trying to communicate with Shauna.

After one of my shots I looked over, Gav was possibly getting blown out. I laughed, but John's demeanour became more serious as he explained.

"The girls belong to the bar, if you want to get to know them better you have to pay a bar fine – and be careful, not all the girls are girls, if you know what I mean."

I nodded my understanding and laughed a little more at Gav. John continued the serious tone, "And the bar is owned by the Mafia... If you win the 20 games, you will get beaten up and thrown out. They broke the jaw of the last winner – be careful."

After a little more fun watching Gav, I quietly mentioned that Shauna was a hooker, and could conceivably be Shaun. We lost the next game and went on our merry way without being black-balled by Don Gan. We never did find out if it was Shauna, or Shaun. Gav and I agreed that either way, she was stunning!

We frequented several more bars along the Koh San Road, largely without any further excitement, but with plenty of cheap local liquor. We met a few helpful travellers, who were more than happy to talk to us about where to go, what to do and see. I realised the six Lonely Planets I was lugging around would be largely unnecessary.

Around 2 a.m. we were about to get a taxi back to the very fancy hotel, when Gav exclaimed, "I am hungry – let's get some food."

A good night in the UK more often than not ended up with a kebab or a pizza in the cab home. He had spotted some food carts. "Ah, street food – I read about these things – let's go eat." We went over to see what was on offer; a little worse for wear, it took us a while to realise that the stall was offering deep fried cockroaches. We took a pass and looked at the next one - scorpions. We looked at each other wide-eyed and without needing any words turned to go look somewhere else.

As we waited to cross back towards the bars, a big silver car with tinted windows pulled up. My heart began to race. The window wound slowly down. I was relieved to see that it wasn't the Don Gan coming to cut Gav's finger off. It was two sweet young ladies.

The driver beckoned us over. I stepped to the window and put my head inside. Both ladies had short skirts and looked like they had been dressed for a club, not the backpacker bars.

I instantly knew the driver was classy as she had a can of beer propped open between her legs. I asked if they didn't have drinking and driving laws in Thailand.

She shrugged and laughed. "We don't care, we are from

Cambodia, and I am princess so they can't touch me." She continued, "Party, get in".

I wondered why having a name like Princess would preclude one from the very long arm of the Thai law. During the drive it was established that she was some sort of royalty – a real princess! Her name was Wan.

"Pleased to meet you, Wan," I said. "I never met a Cambodian princess before."

In fact, I had never met anyone from Cambodia before. Furthermore, I wasn't even sure where Cambodia was. What I did know was that she was beautiful.

She introduced us to her 'friend', who it turned out was her 'permanent secretary', a sort of helper for all things while she was having fun in Bangkok. I guess in the 'west' we'd describe her as a kind of servant – it was like something from an Asian version of Downton Abbey.

Princess Wan grabbed my arm and whispered not so quietly, "My fren, likes your fren," and made a pseudo sexual slapping with her hands and giggled – not quite the way I would expect a princess to speak, but when in Rome!

The party was in their suite on the penthouse floor of one of the biggest hotels in Bangkok. I will not name the hotel so as to avoid a lawsuit, or worse.

It was a party for four people. I was okay with that. Gav was nervous. He was always nervous about things.

"Lighten up, dude" I said.

He just went quiet, sat stiffly next to his new 'fren' and drank his beer. The music was pumping and the laughter flowing, when Princess Wan sat on my lap and began kissing me. I looked at Gav – he was not impressed.

Princess Wan then asked us if we wanted to 'smoke'. Gav and I both nodded in the affirmative. I hoped this would relax Gav, but he often got more paranoid when he smoked weed. The Princesses Servant went to the fridge and got out a white vial containing a black substance. I thought it must be posh Asian hash that needs to be in the fridge, as maybe the heat sends it bad. I wondered if she'd smuggled it in from home, like Gav would have done, or bought it here?- I smiled to myself.

She expertly rolled a joint and lit it, taking a puff herself before passing it around. We all smoked a little. It relaxed me but had no seeming effect on Gav. It made Princess Wan horny. She began to kiss me and quickly started to remove my clothes. My altered state meant I bore no concern for the other people in the room seeing me being de-robed – all I could think was I can't wait to tell my mates I got laid by a Cambodian princess.

But then, just as it all started to heat up, with both of us naked, Wan stopped. A conversation with the maid ensued. What seemed like rushed words were exchanged and the maid shuffled quickly to the bathroom and back. As the maid approached, my self-consciousness rose, fortunately only slightly as, much to my amazement she had come over to help by administering protection.

She expertly slid the condom onto my thankfully still erect penis and silently drifted back towards Gav, who I assumed was still sitting silently on the bed. I was left to concentrate on Wan.

I was not surprised when several, okay maybe it was just a few, moments later, the maid was back to help me clean up! Before I could say "tie a knot in it", the condom was gone and I had been wiped down with a warm towel.

Things had changed in Cambodia after the end of the reign of the Khmer Rouge and Pol Pot. Clearly there was now a more liberal approach, but nothing was more important than retaining the purity of the Cambodian royal lineage, it seemed. If only the Saxe-Coburgs had been so diligent.

No sooner had I slipped my fake Calvin boxers back on, than Gav had seemingly come back to life. There was now urgency in his voice and his movements. We had to leave.

"What? No afterglow?" I grinned gormlessly.

At the same time, Wan was asking, "Why your fren dun' wanna fuk my fren?"

The room was spinning a little and I was getting more and more chilled.

Gav was muttering like a mad man. At one point among the babble, he seemed to say, "They are gonna steal our kidneys, we gotta get out of here, man."

I had had a good night, and if Gav was getting weed paranoia that was fine by me.

"Take me back to our posh hotel," I giggled. I wasn't that bothered about waking up with royalty anyway.

In the private lift down to the lobby, I was still floating in my own little world. Gav was proclaiming a victory, like we had been extracted from behind enemy lines in WWII and saved from a fate worse than death.

We took a cab back to the Koh San Road, as the only taxi man available at the fancy hotel didn't know where our (not quite so) fancy hotel was. The 'rationale' from me was that I could direct the next taxi man from there, back to our hotel. How stoned was I!?!

We sat on the curb at the end of the Koh San Road, directly across from the scorpion vendor, taking a moment to rest before making our next move. It was almost 5 a.m., and it seemed like a sensible thing to do.

Sitting on the curb in Thailand is surprisingly comfy as they are about 18 inches high to cater for the monsoon rains, but also have huge, grateless, gaping holes which lead down to the sewers. In really heavy rains, many of the girls in the pool bar we had frequented could be swept away, never to be seen again. Not a pretty thought.

My lethargy increased – after all it had been a long night already and the roadside seemed like a sensible place to rest up. My eyes were heavy, but not too heavy to spot the road sweeper coming down the street. I laughed. Although it was probably still 50 metres away, I quipped to a still-frantic Gav that we better hurry and get off the road for fear of being swept away.

I mocked him with a game of chicken, refusing to move. The sweeper neared us, and some yelling ensued. I assume that it was a solid instruction to move in Thai – they were clearly not stopping for a stupid farang*.

I acquiesced, well, my mind did. I couldn't move a muscle. It felt like the entire world was pushing down on me. I could barely lift my head. Gav had to jump down onto the road and lift my dead legs up and roll me onto the pavement. He jumped up alongside me just seconds before the sweeper went past where we had been sitting.

SOME THINGS WHICH ON REFLECTION I LEARNED FROM THAT NIGHT:

1. Black weed which is kept in the fridge in a little vial is more commonly called opium and is pretty commonly smoked in Asia and the Middle East.
2. My opium tolerance is low (and has since and will always remain that way).
3. It's better to ask before you smoke – even if you feel like a twat. I would have felt like a bigger twat if I have been swept away by a Thai road cleaner.

*White / Western backpacker, or more generally used term for foreigner.

4. Wan was clearly wealthy but probably not a real princess, probably not even Cambodian. But some lies don't matter.

5. Maybe I still hadn't met anyone from Cambodia.

6. Maids only become expert condom rollers with practice – I wasn't special!

7. She was definitely Wan, not Ewan. We may not have met a Cambodian, but we had not met a ladyboy (but we wouldn't have to wait long for that!).

Chapter 7 — (more) Mind-Bending Bangkok...

Not deterred by my inadvertent dalliance with opioids a few days prior, Little Gav had gone to meet our 'friends', a Danish couple, to pick up some dope - he was keen on a bifter. I was, needless to say, a little more reserved, not wanting to risk being sucked to my death by a Bangkok road-sweeper two days running.

It seems Scandinavian travellers were not only fond of the odd puff on the herb, but were more than willing to help out any naïve Brits who had no clue where to get weed. In England you'd be taking a bigger risk to your health by buying weed than you would by smoking it.

If you actually managed to find someone to 'help you' buy the stuff, you'd likely be stabbed, robbed or arrested on your way home, so 'borrowing' a bud or two from the Scandis was always the way forward. That was until we met our Canadian friends in Melbourne, which changed the game, with almost terminal consequences; but that's for later.

Little Gav beamed like the Cheshire cat as he held up a little clear bag; you know, the ones with the air-tight sealing strips that are all but impossible close properly.

It reminded me of the ones we used to take our dinner money in, back in primary school: as you did in 1986. If you have no idea what I am going on about (as you are under 40), It's like a very small sandwich bag, stuffed with the most pungent smelling weed we had ever experienced – some good the seal did.

"This is gonna be good," giggled Gav.

"Fuck me," I snorted with laughter. "Giggling already? Did you smoke one on your way back?" We fell about laughing.

A few puffs on the dutchie and we were suitably high. Thai weed was living up to its reputation as incredibly strong – that being said, I had little to benchmark it against, but, again, when in Rome!

We were not about to stay in floating around the hostel, so we headed out in search of some fun. Gav brought along another joint for later!

We giggled and tried to navigate the stairs, our co-ordination somewhat lacking. As we stumbled merrily out onto the street, we were faced with our first hilarious dilemma. Which way should we turn?

We giggled left into one of the quiet sois* and immediately took a right onto a slightly wider street with an unpronounceable name. The noise of the backpacker district was still a block away, when we were brought to a sobering halt.

"Shawzy," Gav said almost in a hush, "do you see that?".

"Yeah dude," I drawled, wide-eyed and a little gormlessly.

*A street with no name- I wonder if Bono got his inspiration in Bangkok?

"So, I am not hallucinating then?" Gav continued.

"Nope, not unless I am too," my attempted humour belying my growing fear.

We stood still, barely daring to breath. We had found ourselves face to face with a gigantic bull elephant, just trundling along the city street.

"Keep still," I urged as the beast plodded towards us. "If you run, it will chase us," I asserted. "I watched David Attenborough, dude, stay still."

"Fuck Attenborough, Shawzy, if we stay still it's gonna plough right into us."

I barely heard the end of Gav's sentence as he dived for the safety of the nearest Soi. I was in hot pursuit.

Breathless, some 20 or 30 metres up the side street we turned back to see if the elephant we had run away from was in fact real. Bent double, resting arms on knees we looked up, gasping for air only, to see another elephant; confused but also relieved that this one was being gently persuaded along by its 'owner'. Apparently, taking your elephants for a walk is what you do on a Tuesday night in Bangkok.

All the adrenaline and the dope called for a beer. We had a couple of big Bintangs, but the night never really got going after that. So, earlier than normal, we decided to call it a night. On the way back to the hostel, that twinkle came to Little Gav's eyes again, as he produced the other joint.

All I could think was, how the fuck had he kept that in his jeans pocket all night without breaking it? He smoked as we walked down the street – I declined. He took this as some kind of personal affront, like I was challenging him, taking his efforts to get the weed for granted? I don't know. Anyway, rather than chill him out, it made him paranoid, which was a fairly regular occurrence for him when stoned.

He huffed and puffed, mumbling incoherently as we swayed along the street. He became more and more agitated and as we neared the hostel, I tried my best to calm him down. Then, I made the mistake of putting my arm around him as a gesture of solidarity. He flung my arm away, citing some further disgust at my refusal to smoke.

Like the good friend I am, I just laughed at him, letting out several of my biggest, deepest belly laughs. As my mind drifted, I thought of our conservative friends we had left behind and continued to laugh at the hilarity of two 'working-class' English lads on the lash in Bangkok then, thwack, I felt something thud into my jaw. An intense pain shot across my face. Momentarily I was dazed but quickly got myself together to see Gav next to me rubbing his knuckles. He had punched me!

I should have known that my reaction to the punch would not calm the situation, as not 30 seconds earlier, I had had the necessary lesson, but instinctively I burst out laughing. Bangkok really was mind bending.

Now, it's probably a good juncture to explain that Little

Gav is called *Little* Gav for a reason. Not because we have two friends called Gav and he is the smaller of the two, nor is it some kind of irony like Little John from Robin Hood, who was a brute. No. Little Gav is just very small. Five-foot-five and probably 65kg, wet through. I, on the other hand was 85kg and had at least six inches more than Gav (and six inches of additional height!). It was a mismatch. I also had the added benefit that I had not smoked since we had escaped from the elephants a few hours earlier.

Odds against, Gav lunged forward with another punch. I swayed out of the way gracefully (if I do say so myself), coming to rest as I slammed hard into the wall. Being nimble, Gav managed to swivel, rather quicker than anticipated, and came at me again. This time with a rugby tackle to the waist. He drove the air out of my lungs so I couldn't shout to call him off. We grappled for what seemed like an eternity, but was probably more like five or six seconds. With all my might I pushed back against him. I was getting the upper hand, when we both just flopped onto the floor.

Whether we were too tired, too stoned or just came to our senses, the fight was over. I can only imagine what it's like to grapple for 'five rounds of five minutes with Conor McGregor! We lay on the floor in the lobby of the hostel and burst out laughing. We were joined in our laughter by the three or four astonished backpackers and the receptionist in the lobby, who up until that point, we had been blissfully unaware of even having been there!

As we lay on our backs laughing, Gav turned his head to

look at me and exclaimed, "I could have had you there."

We all laughed louder.

Chapter 8 — Let the 'Real' Backpacking Begin

So, after a few days in Bangkok of pushing every envelope more aggressively than a schizophrenic postmaster, we decided it was time to head to a beach and chill for a bit. But we were backpacking, bang up for more parties and this was Thailand in 2001– chances of a chill out not likely, but like many things, it seemed like a good idea at the time.

We were heading to Krabi and Phuket, but the night before we were due to leave Bangkok, some hippie chick with filthy clothes and several facial piercings persuaded us to change tack and go to Ko Samet. She was not really our type of traveller, so no idea why we even listened to her advice, but we did.

Ko Samet is a small island off southeast coast of Thailand as you head towards Cambodia, and it sounded absolutely idyllic. No cars and very few residents. A few beach shacks serving as hotels, and a plethora of beach bars dashed up and down the stunning shimmering white sand beach which runs the entire length of the island. And there were lots of backpackers, which meant young, nubile females in skimpy bikinis. Perfect.

From Bangkok, it is only a three-hour coach ride to the port town of Rayong and a 45-minute hop in a boat from there. Much easier than getting a flight to Phuket, you'd think.

For the only time we were away together, Little Gav had

looked something up in the Lonely Planet. He had found Pattaya! Now Pattaya was not like it is today – the full scale of debauchery had not yet been realised – but the high-rises were already starting to sprout up, and it was still known for being a party town right on the beach. It didn't take long to be persuaded to 'break-up' the journey to Ko Samet.

With hotel booked and coach ticket purchased, we waited at the central bus station. It was hot. Very hot. It was Boardies and flip flops weather. I eschewed the wife beater for a standard T, as the coaches were renowned for their arctic- strength air-conditioning. A T-shirt would have to suffice as it was the warmest bit of kit I owned. I hadn't yet acquired my fisherman's pants or a pashmina.

With an hour to kill before departure, we picked at some greasy 'meat' pastries, which seemed to be on sale at every corner. As far as I can tell, they are described as 'meat' for one of two reasons. Either 1) no-one knows what kind of meat or combinations of meat is in it or 2) the clever marketing department realise if they are too obtrusive then that might hurt sales. If advertised, you probably wouldn't willingly eat a dog pastry as a pre-road-trip snack.

As we sat stifled, stuffed and swatting flies, CRAMP, my stomach churned. And again. I delicately sipped on my full-fat Coke, hoping it would work its magic. You can't beat a real Coke when you are dehydrated, hungover or just want something to settle you down. I didn't think it was going to work in time, so I headed for the loo. I avoided the 'third gender' toilets which would have been noteworthy back in 2001, and found the men's room.

It was worse than any football stadium loo I have ever been to, in fact it was worse than a festival toilet on a Sunday lunchtime. The floor was swimming, an inch deep in 'dirty water'. Gingerly I stepped in, my stomach growling. I tried to block out the gentle lap of liquid on my ankle bones.

I pushed the first door open; "Sawasdee" came the voice of the little man crouched over with his back to me, curling one out. I almost chundered. I was never going to unsee that! The fourth stall was delightfully unoccupied. I stepped inside. I was resigned to the fact I would have to squat but I hadn't factored for the no bog roll. The only thing in the little cubicle with me was a bowl. That too was full of filthy water. I had a dilemma.

I could take a shit, washing my arse with my hand, using filthy water in a plastic bucket that a hundred other hands had used to 'wash' their filthy arses, or I could hold on. Up came the Boardies, and I made haste back to the bench to find Gav. I rinsed my feet off with bottled water and resigned myself to wait 20 more minutes. I would use the loo on the coach. I needed to be careful though, as there was little room for error. Underwear was not part of the backpackers' uniform. Not ideal but I dug in.

When the time came, we were ushered towards our transport and a little Thai man grabbed our backpacks like they weighed the same as an anorexic's lunchbox and tossed them into the boot of a very compact 12 seat minivan.

I began to protest, but I was assured that this indeed was the 'coach' for Pattaya. I realised, just about as quickly as you have, that 12 seat minivans do not have onboard toilets. I took a deep breath and held it. That was probably the most uncomfortable three hours of my life; the hotel facilities with a real flush toilet, a seat and loo roll was like heaven when we finally got to Pattaya. I pity anyone who was in that room at the same time – it was violent!

Chapter 9 — Hookers, Ladyboys and Just Little Boys

In a land renowned for its idyllic white sand beaches and clear turquoise seas, we had managed to find a place with a fake beach, and a sea overrun by jet-skis and other diesel driven vessels, creating an oily slick on top of the water and a danger of being run-over if you ventured more than 5 metres from shore. Welcome to the paradise that is Pattaya.

We had paid for three nights at a 4-star hotel in advance. It was a bit of a comedown from the ultimate luxury of Bangkok, but it was nice enough. The hotel receptionist looked at us as we checked in.
"You Gay?" she asked.

"I am Gav – G-A-V" he chuckled. "How did you know my name?"

She looked blank. Then with a hint of realisation she re-worded the question, "You bum-bum boys?" making a fist and whacking it into her other palm.

"Fuck off, no!" Gav retorted.

"Well, you cannot share room."

Some minutes later we had managed to be allowed to share a room, under the strict instructions we only brought one bird back at a time. *"What kind of hotel is this?"* I thought.

Flushed with the relief of a flushing toilet, we settled into our room. Later we headed out for dinner where there were a few foreigners dotted around the main drag, but it was mainly Thais in skirts. We were getting excited.

"I can see why they wanted us to get separate rooms now!" I exclaimed.

Gav just laughed and rubbed his hands together.

Over dinner we got chatting to a middle-aged British guy who, by the depth of his tan, had been in Thailand for at least a decade, and had missed the slip-slap-slop ad campaign. We were white as sheets and very green.

He wanted to help show us the way, explaining that the girls are all available; he almost blew our minds. But he warned, "There's a couple of things you young bucks need to know. The girls will all want money. They are not hookers, per se, they are just making a living and a nice caring boyfriend is expected to help out, even if it's for just one night."

Not put off by this, Gav replied, "You said a couple of things – they want paying to fuck, but what's the other?"

A smirk came across his face. He said, "Some of them have cocks."

Gav and I almost choked on our Singhas*.

*Another type of beer (we were becoming connoisseurs).

Sometime later, composure regained, Gav asked our friendly uncle how to tell if it was a lady-boy or not. "You just gotta ask – they won't mind," came the reply.

With that, it was game on. Gav decided the best way to honour the hotel's request was to get cracking straight away.

Chatting away to a skinny but somewhat tall 'chick' at the bar, I was assuming he was asking the two important questions. In no time he was back to the table to ask for the room key and off he went. It was 8 p.m. He was back in an hour with a big smile on his face.

"So?" I enquired, "How was it?"

"Fucking sensational," was his only reply.

We didn't get much sleep later that night, as we had another visitor. This one was seemingly included in the room rate and it definitely had a cock. It also had four legs.

We heard it first, patter, patter, patter, then we felt, thud, as it landed close to our heads. It was a rat! Not any old rat. A fucking huge rodent, like something from the Teenage Mutant Ninja Turtles movie. It was so fat it had fallen off the air-con pipe attached to the wall, directly over the bed. Our screams sent him running for cover and he dived into a pile of our dirty clothes in the corner of the room. We stood on the bed throwing things at his temporary hide-away until eventually we forced him to retreat. He blubbered up the pipe like Chubby Checker doing the twist and disappeared from view through a tiny hole into the ceiling void.

The following day, with our moral compasses having been well and truly shaken, we decided to take it steady. We walked along the strip looking for a suitable place for dinner, one where we wouldn't be accosted by the locals looking to supplement their pocket money on a Friday evening.

Then we saw the oasis in the desert we had been looking for. The Hard Rock Café. I was sure this would provide us the refuge we needed, and we quickened the pace. As we neared, Gav said he was worried we didn't have enough money for the night.

I remembered, on the way out we had limited our pocket cash as a way to avoid further deviancy that evening. The rest of our money and traveller's cheques were securely locked away in the safe deposit box back at the hotel.

We shrugged and vowed we'd be careful to not over-order food. With a to grin Gav mused, "At least this will keep us on the straight and narrow tonight."

We toasted that with a bottle of Bud*, which was four times the cost of a Singha next door. We were happy for the air-con and the refinement.

*if you don't know that this is another type of beer, I think you might be reading the wrong book.

But, before we had even had a chance to order our Manhattan Burgers, we noticed that the clientele were a bit odd. Previously overwhelmed by the ratio of women to men in Pattaya, we slowly became aware that we were in a room with 99% men.

To be more accurate it was 99% male, as many of the Thais who accompanied the big fat Caucasians could probably not legally be described as men.

Some were probably a third of the age of their dates and likely a quarter of their weight. A multi-cultural family bonding session this was not. We immediately left to battle the hawking hookers once again.

We chose an open-air bar for the very reason that it was quiet, and immediately ordered food and some beers. We needed to wash away our disgust. Not long after the food arrived and as if from nowhere, a line-up of about ten hotties came from a previously unnoticed back room and approached the table. They were all above 6ft and wearing feather boas.

Gav nudged me and whispered, "I reckon they are trannies."

"No shit, Sherlock," I sniggered.

We were fascinated. They were beautiful. I mean stunning. Like models. One resembling a pale-skinned Naomi Campbell sat on my knee and began chatting to us as we tried to eat our Pad Krapow and Green Curry. We had a good bit of banter; they were really funny and spoke great English. After Naomi started trying to stroke my cock, we politely made it clear we were not going to be partaking and they left us alone without issue.

We enjoyed the rest of the evening, the banter mainly surrounding how big Naomi's cock would have been and how much Gav would have to pay me to find out!

We had never even seen a transsexual before, let alone talked to one. We left richer for the experience and less poor for not indulging in the experience.

We made it all the way back to the hotel without further incident, well, almost all the way back! With the hotel's front door in sight, Gav announced he had 60THB left (about £1.00 in 2001) and that we could get a whole bucket of beers for 50THB in the bar right next door. What could go wrong? We went in.

Like most of the bars, it was seemingly just us, until we entered. We were the only patrons for sure. And just as predictably as the daffodils coming out in spring, a line-up of beautiful ladies popped out from a room behind the bar. Gav ordered the bucket of beers and did a verbal gender appraisal. These girls were petite, feminine and spoke more alto than baritone but that still wasn't a guarantee.

A bucket consists of five beers. After two each, Gav dived into the fifth one, proclaiming, "Ha, too slow!" It was almost 1 a.m. and I was whacked so didn't fight him for it. But that was the straw that broke the (very weak) camel's back. After just two games of Connect Four he was in love with the bar girl and had a conundrum. The 'bar fine' to take her out of work was 500TBH. It wasn't so much the moral conundrum this time, more a practical one. He had no money. After 10pm, hotel reception prohibited access to the deposit boxes where his money was stored. What to do? Well, blag it, of course. He left the bar like the Terminator, uttering Arnie's inimitable words, "I'll be back."

He arrived back 10 minutes later, looking like the lovechild of the Cheshire Cat and a wide- mouthed frog. Devilment in his eye, he slapped the 500THB on the bar. and shrugged at me, saying, "I said it was an emergency, so they let me into the safe box."

Emergency now over, he was about to walk back past that same receptionist with the bar girl from next door. Another hour of Connect Four for me – thankfully the girls took pity on me and gave me a free beer to help pass the time.

Pattaya had been like a strong magnet on our moral compasses, and we needed to stop spinning, so a day earlier (and two days later) than originally planned, we headed for Ko Samet.

Chapter 10 — One of My Favourite Places on Earth

Ko Samet was truly all it was cracked up to be. Absolutely stunning and still one of my favourite places on Earth. It was chilled out but fun. The sun shone, the beach was like no other, well maybe not the best ever, but better than Pattaya anyway! The crystal-clear waters lapped gently against the brilliant white sand. It was indeed idyllic.

We were due to arrive on the last boat, which, according to the schedule, was set for departure at 2 p.m. Being the responsible tourists we were, we arrived a whole hour early so as not to miss it. We needn't have bothered. We boarded at 3 p.m., but then waited another 90 minutes for the last sack of rice, chickens, stray dog and lobster bucket to be loaded. As the sun sank low over the ocean to the west, the boat sank slightly in the water and we finally cast off.

As we chugged out of the harbour, which was only discernible as such by a few big stones poking out of the sea, the slight swell was depositing some water inside the boat. Our first thought was to go down below deck, get our backpacks and bring them to higher 'ground', but alas that was not going to happen as they were well and truly buried under what looked like a year's supplies for this tiny island.

As we bobbed along, at the mercy of Poseidon (or the Thai equivalent), the mild fear of a wet backpack was replaced by a visceral fear that we might actually sink. Gav was not a great swimmer. This long, thin wooden creation was coughing and spluttering over, and frequently under, the still small waves. What looked like a 15cc outboard motor powering the vessel, seemed older than time itself and was depositing about the same volume of grease into the sea as the water we were taking onboard. An eco-voyage this was not.

Our fears never materialised. We had one up on the Titanic. The sun had now set, and we knew we had arrived when the boat thudded into the dock. We waited and waited, for what seemed like an eternity for our bags to be thrown off the boat. It was pitch black by the time we finally left port in search of a hotel. My trusty Maglite was at the bottom of my bag, and I decided against the 20-minute 'unpack – repack' needed to access it.

With no vehicular access on the island, we agreed to go to the nearest 'hotel', stay there for the night and explore our options more fully the following day. We could then rest our weary heads and not need to lug our backpacks unnecessarily all the way down the beach in the dark.

We walked into what, even in the dark, looked like a ramshackled hovel. I have never been a fussy sleeper, but on Gav's insistence, we had the hotel manager show us first, before coughing up the £3 for the room. No sooner had I tossed my bag on the bed and sat down, a shrill shriek had me back on my feet.

I followed the blood-curdling noise into the dimly-lit bathroom where I saw a white-faced Gav staring into the loo. It was a proper western loo, with a seat, but this couldn't be the reason for the scream, surely? Granted it was avocado (yeah – just like your mum's bathroom was in the 80s) but it seemed like an overreaction.

I peered into the darkness and there it was, a gigantic blue and orange insect (?) that resembled a millipede on steroids glowing back up at us. It took up half the bowl. At that moment I needed to use the very same loo that was being occupied by this unknown creature, but before you could shout 'flush it away', in a violent flash the insect was gone, viciously gobbled up by what looked like a scorpion, which then also disappeared into the darkness. Just like the bus journey, I squeezed my butt cheeks and held on tight.

To this day, that's the only hotel/hostel room I have ever rejected. We ended up staying in the next hotel down the beach! It was a relative paradise, but I didn't dare sit on their throne either.

The following day we found our haven. A wooden shack on stilts set into the hill. It was 'marketed' as an eco-lodge and maybe off-set the carbon footprint of the boat ride. It had wooden floors, a massive bed (just one), a bathroom free from unknown critters and even a little balcony. We were set. We sat out on the balcony with a beer as the sun set. It was absolutely class. We clinked glasses and relaxed.

After a beer or two Gav enquired, "Do we have any mozzie spray?"

"Tiger Balm," was my reply, "in the bathroom. Bring it out 'ere when you come." There were a few big mozzies buzzing around so it seemed like a good time to don some of the world's most potent insect repellent.

Tiger Balm in 2001 was not as it is these days. In fact, the Thai labelled stuff was banned from being exported to many countries as it was deemed unsafe for human use. It did the job for us, for the most part! We headed out to a nearby beach hut for some dinner and a mini bucket of Sang Som*. A couple of hours later we returned to the hut for our first early night since leaving Barnsley.

On our return, we took care not to let the mozzies into the room as we entered, but upon turning the light in we found, to our dismay, we had already been infiltrated. Although the windows had screens on them, most of which were fit for purpose, there were gaping chasms between several of the lengths of wood used to build the floor of the place. We opted for more Tiger Balm and hit the hay.

We awoke to glorious sunshine, which had heated up our eco-lodge to somewhere close to 40 degrees, and the humidity meant that even flaring a nostril could induce a flood of sweat.

We headed to the beach to sleep some more. It was 6:45

*local rum served in a mini-bucket usually with Thai RedBull for an extra kick!

a.m. The mozzies had headed home long before that, having thoroughly gorged on our blood. More Tiger Balm was applied to stop the itching.

I sunbathed in the glorious dry heat, cooled off in the pan-flat, clear blue sea, lounged under palm trees reading Harry Potter, nibbled on a sumptuous Pad Thai Goong* and ended the afternoon with a four-hands massage on the beach. I paid less than £10 for an hour of pure bliss and was so zen I left my sunglasses on the massage mat. My faith in humanity remained intact when one of the little Thai ladies came chasing me up the beach to hand back to me, possibly the only real pair of Oakley's in Thailand!

Backpacking is the only commonality needed to induce conversation almost anywhere, with anyone. Even the most introverted souls got themselves out there, and I was humbled to speak to literally hundreds of people I would never have otherwise spoken to that year.

There were plenty of weirdos and oddballs, but that was some of the fun. Not everything you were told was absolutely true, and not all the advice offered was useful but much of it was. We were very glad to get chatting to an Israeli guy that day.

He was a bit of a know-it-all type, which bristled my 24-year-old alpha self, but it would have been bad form to just tell him to fuck off, we weren't in Barnsley now, as Gav would frequently remind me.

*King Prawn noodle and beansprout dish delicately encased by an egg lattice.

So, Gav and I were only half-listening when a mozzie bit Gav on the finger. Swat. Got the bastard.

Our new friend got excited and animatedly burst into a diatribe, "Ah, they are big here, the mozzies. Did you know they introduced these giant mozzies to eat all the ones who carried malaria? They successfully got rid of the malaria, but these fuckers don't half leave a big lump when they bite. Did you get a mozzie ring for your room?"

I wondered if this was a Hebrew euphemism.

It turned out to be a (mainly) true story, and he went on to explain that the ring wasn't a sinister Mossad sex toy but in fact, you could buy a little green ring made of what looked like cardboard, which, when lit with a match, gave off a very subtle single plume of barely visible smoke. This was purportedly enough to keep the mutant mosquitos at bay.

He pointed to one under Gav's chair. Several of them were keeping the open-air bar clear and he assured us that putting just one in the room was the best way to not get bitten at night. Buoyed by this we bade him farewell and returned to the hut, via the store. A pack of 10 green mozzie repelling rings in hand, we headed home and got ready to go out for dinner.

We set up one of the rings and positioned it at the bottom of the bed. After 10 minutes, we were reassured that it wasn't burning enough to burn the hut down and we were about to leave. Then, we noticed that the ring was hardly giving off any smoke and agreed it might not be sufficient to repel such massive insects in our sizeable room. So, we put two more in the bedroom, one in the bathroom and one outside the door on the balcony. Reassured that we would later enjoy a fantastic night's sleep, we headed out for the night.

A few beers and some fantastic food followed. The fried fish tasted like it had been cooked in extra virgin olive oil and not extra slutty boat engine oil which was another bonus. We were happy and chilled, settling into this travelling lark. With a tired glow from the sun, a buzz from the beer, we jovially headed back to the hut ready to crash out.

Our expectations of a nocturnal nirvana were shattered upon entering the hut. We were immediately met with a wall of smoke. Fearful that the place was burning down, we dashed inside to save our bags and passports, if nothing else (something I wouldn't be able to do in Queensland a few months later).

Panic over. There was no fire. There were also no mozzies either. That said, the smoke from the five rings we had placed around the room hung thick and putrid. It tore at our throats as we inhaled, and it was immediately obvious that we couldn't sleep there until we had 'aired out' the room. Wafting towels around trying to disperse the fog proved futile. Off to the beach we went! It wasn't actually a bad slumber and despite a few bites we woke relieved not to have been eaten alive.

On a subsequent night, I got chatting to a 30-something-year-old lady named Grace. I was into older women, so she seemed perfect. Come to think of it, I was into all women, without any hint of ageism, mysogyny or discrimination – all women were to be treated equally. I was years ahead of my time. Being totally honest though, Grace was beautiful.*

We chatted and laughed, and she seemed to genuinely like me, so I was disappointed when she said she was calling it a night. She then tricked me into walking her home. She recounted a disturbing tale from the previous night where she had walked home alone, accompanied only by the eerie feeling that someone was following her. I took the bait, stood, and chivalrously presented my hand.

I wouldn't say she raped me exactly, but she was many years my senior and she certainly knew what she was doing. As I lay there in the afterglow, I realised much to my joy that her bed had a mozzie net around it. Double win! I fell into a deep, dreamless sleep, a happy man, only to wake to find my feet had been stuck out the bottom of the net all night and my lower legs had been devoured like the fatted calf at Nero's ultimate orgy.

Despite our schoolboy errors, we were having a blast. It was less hectic than Bangkok, which, if we had stayed any

And even if she wasn't, this is my book and as my mate Dan told me many a time – never let the truth get in the way of a good story!

longer, might just have killed us. We had eased happily into the lazy days on the beach and the chilled-out evenings.

The people on the island were bohemian. We met loads of backpackers, some who I would keep re-meeting all around the world. We met locals who worked on the island and some who lived in Rayong. I wouldn't fancy that rickety boat commute every day. We also met several expats, mainly EFL* teachers, but it made me think about working in Thailand – a dream I would fulfil some 15 years later.

All the bars and restaurants were open-air and either directly on or just set back from the beach. We ate an array of fish and other sea creatures plucked straight out of the sea that very day. The flavours were amazing; lemongrass, chilli, fresh coconut cream, fresh coriander, which talented chefs turned into aromatic dishes such as Pad Thai Goong, Krapow, and a plethora of curries originally named after their colours, red, green and massaman.

I know, massaman is not a colour, but it's brown, and it seems that the massaman company has the same marketing advisors as the meat pastry people we encountered earlier. You wouldn't call your dish brown curry now, would you?!

We were lucky enough to be on Ko Samet for a full

English as a Foreign Language

moon party. It wasn't a true full moon party, as it was actually only a quarter moon but that didn't stop anyone from having the same amount of fun as you would at a full, full moon party. It was on a long and lonely bus journey across Canada that I realised those marketing geniuses had been at it again. There was a quarter-full moon party every week.

After enjoying more of this amazing food, washed down by a Chang* or three (Ko Chang was the nearest major island and the only brewery between us and Cambodia), we were treated to a fire show and encouraged to drink 'Sang Som buckets'.

Sang Som is like a whiskey/brandy made in Thailand and it's very strong. It was mixed with Thai Red Bull, which, like the Tiger Balm, is a much more robust cousin of the watered-down version we get in the west. And why is it called a bucket, I hear you ask? It's served in an actual bucket – like the thing kids make sandcastles with.

We ordered one each, and with a smirk the bartender asked, "Do you want the 'worm' as well?"

I knew that bottles of tequila in Latin America often had a worm in the bottom of the bottle and they were rumoured to be hallucinogenic, but I hate tequila and had never had the chance to try one.

I was sceptical but thought fuck it, you only live once, at

Another beer brand!

which point I quickly instructed Little Gav to get me to a hospital if the shit hit the fan.

In the end we had a fantastic evening. Lots of brilliant tunes from the live DJs and MCs, met some great people from all around the world, dancing like they were as free as the day they were born. Mindful of the potency of the 'buckets' we slowed down after that first chug. We were fully chilled though, and at some stage in the night we had moved our wicker chairs the ten or so metres to sit in the calm shallows of the sea.

The water lapping at our feet, soft as a feather duster and as cool as The Fonz, was blissful. I had hardly noticed the effects of the worm until the point where I asked Gav, "Is it ever going to get dark?"

"It's 7:30 in the morning," came his incredulous reply. He looked into my eyes and just laughed – he muttered something about pupils the size of dinner plates and zoned back out.

We savoured this wonderful place during our last days in Thailand. Next stop Indonesia, and the beaches of Bali....

Chapter 11 — "Dude, Where's my Watch?"

We landed at Denpasar Airport on the southern tip of Bali, hustled through a cacophony of noise in Arrivals, and finally stepped out of the claustrophobic terminal building into the infernal heat of the day. It was 10 a.m., but the time makes little difference as it's always hot on the equator. Sweat poured from my brow.

I bartered hard with the taxi driver, getting the fare down from £9.06 to £8.25. It was still a 'gazillion Rupiah'. The harum scarum dash through the mid-morning traffic was like some real-life version of Grand Theft Auto. Finally, the roller coaster stopped. Stepping back into the heat, a little green around the gills, I duly tipped the taxi man, at least the 81p that I'd bartered down some 30 minutes earlier. At least the cab had had air-con.

Gav and I were becoming seasoned travellers. Watch out for the con – we knew the score!

The Taxi Uncle had brought us to our hostel in the surfing Mecca of Kuta, which, was highly fashionable in the Christmas of 2001. At the very same time we arrived in Bali, somewhere in cave in Central Asia, a plot was being hatched to kill backpackers just like us. Al Qaeda bombed the Sari Club and adjacent Paddy's Bar just 10 months later, after which, Kuta's popularity unsurprisingly waned.

A little more than a year since 9/11, I would watch, horrified, on a tiny Fijian TV, with 100 or so other backpackers, as the events of 12 October 2002 unfolded: my two Aussie mates, frantically trying to reach their girlfriends; who were on a bachelorette party in Kuta. It made little sense to me, and as egregious as the Twin Towers bombings had been, it had not felt as close to home as this. It was scary. Thankfully, the bachelorettes would not be among the 202 innocent victims of that horrific day. There but for the grace of God go I – as they say.

Our time in Bali was a wonderful, yet mind-blowing experience, even without any thought of suicide bombers, but almost 20 years on it still makes me shiver to think of the terror.

We had two weeks in paradise, before we would head off to Australia on Christmas Eve, where the main backpacking journey would commence in Melbourne. The plan was a Christmas Day beach BBQ and Boxing Day drinking 'VB'* with 90,000 other hungover loons at the MCG, watching Brett Lee try to knock the heads off a bunch of beefcake farmers from South Africa. But we had to navigate Indonesia first...

We had thought Bangkok was still developing and somewhat lacking in 'Western comforts', but Bali was an

*Victoria Bitter or VB as it is fondly shortened to is the local Melbournian drink of choice for the discerning Aussie bloke (and many of the Sheila's too)

even bigger culture shock. Roads, houses and even whole resort hotels were abandoned half completed and there were shanty towns and signs of poverty literally everywhere – but the overriding sense was that the people were happy. The dichotomy between the 'haves' and the 'have nots' was stark - everything was either extremely basic or a five-star resort.

Obviously, we were staying in the basic accommodation category, and when we found out that a twin room with 'air-con' simply meant a queen-sized bed and leaving the window open, we opted for a dorm room with a fan. Our first dorm room.

We checked in and slung our backpacks on the bed, thinking about getting a beer. It was noon, but as the saying goes, it's always 5 p.m. somewhere in the world, and I had read that Nasi Goreng was best enjoyed when washed down with an ice cold Bintang beer – who was I to argue?

Our bellies rumbled with the urge to eat but we had traveller's cheques, a camera, minidisc player, and our passports, wallets and watches to consider. None of which could be left in a dorm room, so we needed a safe deposit box.

Our hostel was not as 'sophisticated' as the hotel in Pattaya. The 'safe' looked rather like one of those Ikea bookshelves with little individual coloured boxes you'd use to keep kids toys in. Access to the box was to simply slide it out using the obliging cotton loop handle. Not very safe and certainly not locked!

The only thing standing (or rather lying down) between our valuables and any 'wanna-be thief' would be a very skinny Indonesian man sleeping in just his pants on a mattress, seemingly 24/7. He was strategically placed directly in front of the bookcase. We hoped he was a light sleeper! And we hoped that our box would be on the bottom row, as access would mean moving the whole mattress not simply reaching out a hand. He gave us a box on the top row.

The upside was that there was no 10 p.m. 'safe-box curfew' as there had been in Pattaya, so if we needed to access 'emergency funds' at 1 a.m., there would be no need to fabricate a situation. We could simply wake up the skinny gatekeeper and ask him for access, or maybe just reach over his snoring body and help ourselves.

We chose carefully which items went inside the 'safe' and decided eventually that we would leave everything except '*spectacles, testicles, wallets and watches*', which would stay on the person at all times. Our valuables deposited, we just looked at each other, shrugged, hoped for the best and headed out for lunch on the much-fabled Kuta beach.

We nestled into a funky little beach bar, sipped on a 'coldy' and gazed longingly as the surf crashed relentlessly against the golden sand. We watched on in awe the tanned and ripped 'chick magnets' skipping along an endless supply of barrels, avoiding the break, diving off as each wave frittered out, resurfacing into view with a shake of their shoulder length hair, like a man's version of a shampoo advert.

Tomorrow we would become surfers, but today we would just enjoy the view and the beers, and rely on our 'legendary' chat to woo the ladies of the Sari Club.

It was Little Gav who proved what would later become my rule of backpacking: that you must have been ripped off in a country to have really 'experienced' it. It was simply not enough to have set foot on the land; that was just a 'visit'.

We didn't waste any time in 'experiencing' Bali; this was our very first day in Indonesia.

Still dreaming of the surf (and the surf-babes), we had a blast that evening, swapping stories with loads of other awesome backpackers. Aussies, Swedes, Germans, Israelis, Palestinians, French and Brits seemed to make up most of the numbers, but we met people from places like Pakistan, Botswana and despite 9/11 even some wary Americans (many of whom prophetically stitched Canadian flags into their backpacks just in case); there was a sense of collective energy in Kuta. It was buzzing.

We visited several of Kuta's plethora of bars, including one with a concrete blue wall shaped like a wave with half a concrete surfboard poking out of it, which, naturally, we stood on like tourists and took pics! We must have looked so cool! After that, about 10 of us headed to the Sari Club, or SC as it was fondly known. Clearly backpackers were too lazy to enunciate the whole three syllables; the name was cut down to two.

SC was an inside-outside kind of place. A sort of beach bar-cum-nightclub, about a mile from the sea on Kuta's main drag. There were no windows or real walls – it was totally open with a patchwork rooves made of thatched straw. The low roof covered the individual tables, bar area and the 'dance floor', which unlike every other dance floor I had ever been on, was a shoes-off affair. It was open until 3 a.m. and all the girls wore bikinis. Right up my street.

Sometime after midnight Little Gav and I decided to call it a night. Slightly merry but far from paralytic, it had been a great night and we tackled the 200m walk along the main street to the hostel. We had no intention of waking up the safe deposit box guard for extra-curricular funding despite the best efforts of two ladies of the night, who seemed to appear from nowhere.

We were literally on the main street. Gav and I just looked at each other. They made no attempt at discretion and were clearly not worried about the plethora of other people, taxi drivers, backpackers, the odd police bike passing by.

I told one of the young ladies in no uncertain terms that I was not interested, despite her clawing at my shirt and following me up the street a little. As I picked up the pace, she finally got the message and disappeared almost as quickly as she had emerged.

I turned to see where Little Gav was. He was some 50 m back. At first, I thought his dick was making the decisions again, but it was clear from the body language that he was looking for an escape route. Chuckling to myself, I enjoyed watching his discomfort and made no move to help!

He was stood with his back to me, and he was shaking his noggin like one of those dashboard bobble-head characters. She was grabbing at his shirt and then trying to hold his hands. I expected his resolve to weaken at any moment, but, just like that, she gave up and walked swiftly away. I laughed out loud.

When Gav caught me up, I poked fun at him and faux-lauded his discipline and resolve and we laughed hard for what little remained of the walk to the hostel. We wondered if the security man would be sleeping in front of our valuables or if the whole hostel had been robbed blind. Much to our relief, our skinny little friend was indeed snoring away, valuables 'securely' protected.

"Not sure why we were so worried," Gav laughed. "Well secure, that!" He pointed at the Ikea shelf.

"Still got your wallet on you?" I joked back.

"Yeah, mate," Gav laughed as he checked his pocket, but his humour was short-lived. He withdrew his hand to reveal a brown arm and a very white, very visible band of skin on his wrist. The white colour on his face matched that of his wrist as he quietly announced, "That hooker has stolen my watch."

The 'lady of the night' hadn't actually been trying to get us to pay for fun and frolics, it was purely a diversion. She had actually stolen his watch, right off his wrist. Grifting of the highest order! We would laugh about this later, but Gav was pretty annoyed at the time. I was just left in awe!

We didn't do very well with watches in Bali.

We went out to buy a replacement for Gav the next day – not to be left out, I decided I wanted one too! Classic FOMO*. We browsed the multitude of fake TAG Heuers, Rolexes and Patek Phillipes. Gav plumped for an Omega, and I went for a big phat TAG.

I had previously owned a TAG, acquired on my first 'lads' holiday to Rhodes in 1995 when I was just 17. I had taken it into a high street jeweller on my return to get links taken out. When the guy at H. Samuel handed me a receipt which read "TAG (Fake)", I was mortified. At least my three-buttoned Ralph Lauren Polos were real.

We paid the princely sum of £5 for each watch. Experienced in the world of fine chronography I recognised they were pretty poor fakes, but at least it wouldn't matter if we got robbed the next night! We left the shop two happy bunnies. Gav's watch fitted perfectly, and I reluctantly admitted it looked great on him.

As we admired it, I joked, "Better not go in the sea in that, I am sure it won't be waterproof."

*Fear of missing out

They must make fake TAGs for weightlifters or professional masturbators, as mine needed at least 4 links taking out. The stall I had bought it from didn't offer the service and I wasn't about to go to H. Samuel, so I looked for an alternative. I was advised to visit a kiosk, which also sold pop, Asian recipe chocolate and condoms, which I would go back another time to buy. Adjacent to the condoms were umbrellas – how random. Keeping both heads dry, maybe. The friendly guy shook his head and sent us about 50 m down a side street, motioning that I should knock on the green garage door. Gav left me to it and went to the pub.

I knocked on the unsigned green garage door as instructed. It slid open with a squeak and a squeal which made me wince, like fingernails on a blackboard. For those of you not old enough to remember blackboards, look up 'misophonia'.

I was welcomed inside by two burly-looking fellas, who clearly spoke no English but seemed friendly as they smiled and shook my hand. It was a multi-purpose engineering kind of place. Dark, with saws, chisels, spanners and spades and a myriad of odds and ends. Across the workshop, a guy was welding a car with just sunglasses on. I was not surprised.

I got my watch out, mumbled something to try and explain why I was there. To my surprise, the bigger guy seemed to be expecting me and pulled out a set of watchmaker screwdrivers. They looked especially tiny in his huge ape-like hands. I amused myself thinking "*this must be the biggest guy in Indonesia – who'd have thought that he'd be so dextrous?"* I was impressed.

I wasn't quite so impressed a few minutes later though. Even though he had skilfully managed to remove the required links, he tried to charge me the equivalent of £15. I told him with some force, that was three times what I had paid for the watch. He just shrugged and held out his hand.

I quickly assessed the situation. The watch was on my wrist, and this was clearly a total scam so in an attempt at 'fairness' I put £2 on the table and began to walk out. The second bounced out of his chair and stepped between me and my exit. I immediately regretted my choice – he was even bigger than the first guy. I stopped in my tracks. He was taller than Jaws from the James Bond films, and equally ugly. I quickly glanced back towards the first beefcake who had by now replaced his watchmakers' screwdrivers with a giant spanner which looked like a suitable tool with which to remove some of the links in my neck.

I quickly reached for my wallet again and grabbed more notes, at least another £15 on top of the two I had already furnished. I held up my hands, one palm open in a gesture of surrender and the other a fist full of Rupiah.

My heart raced. I was frozen to the spot. After what seemed like an eternity the man at the door seemed to soften his stance, a little. He nodded his head and reached out, relieving me of both my wealth and my dignity, and in near perfect English he said, "Lucky boy, this is a Mafia-run place – now fuck off." I sprinted out of the tiny gap in the door, flip-flopping my way back to the safety of the main street!

I treasured that watch; a daily reminder of how close I had come to getting my head kicked in and the need to respect how different cultures work. I carefully removed it every time we went surfing, dutifully rolling it up in a ziplock bag to keep it dry and burying it in the sand so it didn't get stolen. I also took great care not to get it mugged off my wrist in the street.

I would later mull over this tale with Gav as we took off for Australia, looking down on the stunning island we had grown to love, thinking about the beauty and grime, the wealth and the poverty, the haves and the have nots and the Mafia who seemingly controlled the streets and the police. Later in the flight I glanced down to check the time. The TAG has stopped – almost exactly at the time the plane took off! How ironic.

Chapter 12 – Chess Sets and Asian Condoms

Aside from nights in the Sari Club and lazy days spent on Kuta Beach, we saw relatively little of the island. We had enough to do in Kuta, recovering from hangovers and learning to surf! Plus, I can still hear my mum's pleas as I boarded the bus in Barnsley, "Use condoms and don't you dare hire a moped – I want you back in one piece and not riddled with the clap." Quality parenting advice, I am sure you will agree.

We did make one memorable trip and didn't need to hire any kind of bike. We simply hired a car and a chauffeur – albeit inadvertently. Our quest for the day was to go to Jimbaran Bay, which nowadays is adorned with luxury five-star resorts, but in 2001 was known only for its reef break and secluded beach. We hailed a taxi.

Bartering what seemed to be a fair price of £6 with the taxi uncle, we were about to get in, but Gav was rightly worried that we would get stuck in the middle of nowhere, with no chance of getting a ride home. We were about to walk away and give it some more thought, when the driver said, "No problem - I stay with you – come back Kuta when you want."

Incredulous, and feeling another classic scam brewing, we shook our heads and began our retreat. But you don't walk away from a deal that easily in Bali, as I had found out with the watch. He came running after us shouting "not expensive", a classic precursor line to any scam in my experience! But he somehow hooked us in.

"How much?" I asked.

"£10...Me stay all day wit' you," was his reply. After some clarification points, we were on our way.

After a brisk ride out of Kuta, we turned off the main road, thundering over a massive gap in the tarmac, onto what looked like a resort road. The tarmac looked brand-new but was full of cracks and potholes with shrubs growing through. When we got to the car park, and assumed that we were in the wrong place as there was no resort. Clearly, tools had been downed some years ago which seemed a massive shame. It was like a ghost town, where someone had stolen the hotel. Very eerie.

The taxi man helped us get our 'day packs' out of the boot and shooed us off down a dubious-looking path; as we disappeared over the precipice, I checked back and to my surprise he was sat in the passenger side, seat back to the horizontal, feet up on the dash and his eyes covered by his hat! He was clearly going nowhere. Result.

We clambered through the scrub, over rocks and down a steep incline, to be greeted by a stunning, 200m long beach with pure white sand; grains so small it felt like icing sugar. The transparent turquoise sea lapped lazily onto the shore, whispering its seductive charms, tempting us, the only people on the entire beach, to dip in a toe and maybe more. The sun was up high in the cloudless blue sky, shimmered through the haze. A gentle zephyr gave ample respite from the heat as it washed over us. It was majestic. We dropped our bags, took off our wife beaters and headed for the water!

After our swim and ample time to dry off, a couple of locals turned up, seemingly from nowhere. The Balinese were fast becoming the masters of the surreptitious arrival. We couldn't remember seeing any dwellings for miles around. They were intensely tanned with leathery skin from what looked like years of over exposure. They approached us with big toothy grins, offering us bargain-basement-priced refreshments. We duly obliged, as we had turned up thoroughly unprepared, said our thanks and they disappeared.

I have no idea where they went, as there were no other potential customers. We were once again alone. After a couple more hours in this utopia, they returned with a portable homemade BBQ, crafted from half a small oil drum. They also had a line full of freshly caught fish.

We all ate together, sharing the fish. Some corns and flatbreads were passed around. We told stories in broken English with lots of hand gestures and so much laughter. When it was time to leave, they reluctantly accepted a few small Rupiah notes and cheerily waved us off up the hill.

As we ascended the steep slope, up to the deserted resort, I wondered if the locals could have been any happier if the project had been finished. Sure, they would have had hundreds of tourists flooding their beach, providing an endless supply of business, but did they want that? I mused lazily, when Gav whooped and brought me out of my reverie.

To our great surprise, the taxi driver was still there waiting for us! It had probably been a good idea to only pay half up front, but he seemed genuinely delighted with £10 for his day's work. I pondered this too all the way back to Kuta. Economics seemed to work differently here.

We eased into island life with late nights and even later mornings. It's a good job the cafés did 'All-Day-Breakfasts' or we'd have been straight into lunch most days, and occasionally straight to dinner! Days were spent surfing, sunbathing and recovering from the previous night's cocktails – not necessarily in that order. Well, I say surfing, it was mainly getting wiped out by tiny waves, but this was the life.

On our first day of surfing, after a couple of hours on a borrowed surfboard, we were close to being professionals. I almost stood up once and Gav had been on his feet for at least 1.5 seconds. Naturally, we bought our own boards, complete with cases so we could take them to Oz with us. In truth, we were crap at surfing, and they became more of a beach accessory and a talking point at every new hostel, than a serious bit of sports kit The ladies loved them! (Or so we told ourselves.)

When we weren't getting sand-burns and mouthfuls of water after being dumped off the waves, we were pretending to be asleep as the hawkers patrolled the beach selling replacement watches for those of us who had been stupid enough to go in the water in theirs! Gav. I did warn him! For our second week in Bali, Gav wore no watch and I teased him mercilessly when the hawkers had finally left us alone!

The hawkers were local guys, not the 'Looky Looky' types you get in Ibiza or Magaluf. Mostly they were late middle-aged men and would patrol the beach, a different one passing by every 10 minutes. They would stand for ages trying to sell you something, anything. So, the trick was to keep your eyes shut and hope they moved on. It was hard not to feel sorry for them as they laboured all day up and down the beach, lugging with them the entire contents of a traditional seaside store and much more. How they managed it in that heat I will never know.

They proved trickly little suckers to get rid of and, probably through decades of practice, employed a multitude of 'engagement tactics' to establish eye contact. Once made, you were doomed, they wouldn't leave until a sale had been made.

We didn't succumb to the usual chatter where they'd simply name every item they had for sale, but they would use subtle techniques, such as standing in your sun. This created a shadow, cooling the temperature so even if you had eyes closed and hat covering them, it was hard not to want to look up and check if the sun had fallen out of the sky.

This tactic got us a few times but as the quick learners, and the now 'experienced travellers' we were, we wised up to this quickly. Despite this success, one hawker in particular kept getting my attention and despite my attempts to repel him, I simply could not.

His patter was the same every day. Standing in my sun first, I pretended he wasn't there. He would then pipe-up with the usual, "Rrrrrole-lex, Rrrrole-lex, Maruwaaaana, Hasheeeeesh". Annunciating the things his FBI profiling course had clearly suggested I might be most interested in. I remained disinterested in yet more watches and 100% was not buying drugs from a guy on the beach. I remained stoic.

He would continue with, "Condoms, Fanta, sun cream", an odd combination, but probably some kind of pattern interrupt, I thought, as I screwed my eyes tight, trying not to piss myself laughing and waited for him to move on.

Then, just as I thought I was winning the war, he would slowly step out of my sun and utter the fateful words... "Chess set, chess set – one dollar." My eyes involuntarily sprang open, and my head snapped up – he had me.

Every single day, the same outcome.

I was then in for another half an hour of trying to move him on! He was a better salesman than many of the so called 'elite sellers and sales managers' I would go on to train in a later life. He probably earned $10 per day.

The chess sets were stunning, hand carved of polished wood and beautifully finished. They would look fabulous on my home office coffee table in 2021, but this was 2001, and I was a backpacker, with another 11 months living out of a rucksack ahead of me. What the hell did I want with a chess set? It must have been the Yorkshireman in me that couldn't resist a $1 bargain.

I never did buy anything from him at the beach. But, looking back, maybe he had the last laugh by applying the Voodoo curse which stopped my TAG bang on the minute we left the island.

The nightlife in Bali was epic. Everyone was having a blast and for the most part seemed to get along well. One lucky night, I got talking to a Swede called Korolina. A stunningly attractive young lady from Stockholm. She didn't fit my stereotype of a Swede; she was neither blonde nor tall but was heavily tanned and had deep black eyes with a glint of devilment in them.

She was doing the reverse trip to us and was about to head home, but after Bali still had two months in Thailand. She told me many great things about Australia and New Zealand. I was awestruck at the quality of her narrative, especially given it was delivered in a second language. After returning the favour and wooing her with my stories from Thailand – different from the ones I have told you, obviously – she was keen to get 'an early night'.

Immediately regretting that I had not stocked up on protection from the hawker on the beach. I made an awkward stop, at the same kiosk I had bought the watch from, as Karolina waited behind me. We went back to the hostel, shushing and giggling, taking care not to fall over the safe box guard, as he snored loudly like some kind of guard dog in the protection of my passport

Fortunately, we had got in quite early and had the dorm to ourselves, but things did not run 100% smoothly. Some awkward fumbling ensued as I attempted to put a thin layer of latex between us, for both our protection. As gorgeous as a brunette Swede and a blonde Brit combination would be, I certainly did not want to replace the backpack for a carrycot. Nor did I want to tell my mum I had caught the clap.

After the second unsuccessful attempt I gave up, my fingers a sloppy spermicidal mess. Frustrated, the passion had been doused quicker than a fire hose putting out a match. She got dressed, kissed me politely on the cheek and promptly left, never to be seen again. As Shaggy so wonderfully put it "Oh Karolina, Gal yuh feel me jump an' prance (Prowl off, jump an' prance).

I was gutted to say the least and wondered if I should tell Gav the truth or just flat-out lie. As I pondered this moral quandary in the semi-darkness, I mindlessly tidied up the ripped foil packets and unused condoms. It struck me how small they looked. I turned on the main light.

I then remembered someone telling me before we set off to be careful as Durex make a product only sold in Asia. I had presumed that "small rubbers" were an urban myth! I smiled to myself and felt better. I told Gav the truth and never one to miss an opportunity to take the piss, I offered him the remaining johnny, just in case he got lucky!

Bali was a brilliant place for backpackers in 2001 and it still is today. The 2002 bomb had ripped through the SC and the hellish fire, accelerated by the straw roofs and tinder-dry climate had been just as devastating than the bomb itself.

The physical dust settled quicker than the metaphorical dust. The families of those innocent revellers waited six years for some kind of closure, when, in 2008, three of the bombers were convicted and executed by firing squad.

Tourism dipped, as you would imagine but with the amazing resilience of the Balinese, the natural draw of this enigmatic island and some hefty investment in regenerating tourism, Bali now, rightly holds its place once again as one of the top destinations for nomads, artisans, surfers, hippies, luxury holiday makers and backpackers alike.

The main backpacker hub of Canggu is only a mile or so up the coast from the original Sari Club/Paddy's Bar, proving that the human spirit can be deterred but cannot be defeated. Memorials to the 202 people, who were simply in the wrong place at the wrong time, were erected in Kuta and six other locations all around the world.

Chapter 13 — Really 'Experiencing' Australia!

It was Christmas Eve when Gav and I landed at Melbourne's Tullamarine Airport. We were in Australia, and, as five-week travelling veterans, we were relaxed. On the flight in from Bali, we had been lucky enough to get bumped up to Business Class, which has only happened two or three times in the 20 years since, and I have probably taken in the region of 200 flights. I still always ask!

Clearly, the check-in girl who upgraded us fancied me, it can't have been Gav, surely? Or maybe she just had a wicked sense of humour and thought it would be funny to sit a couple of haggard-looking backpackers, a habilimented in the compulsory Boardies and wife beaters next to the expensively-clad Japanese businessman.

Fortunately for Yoshi, it was only a five-hour flight and after the pleasantries were exchanged, I slept like a baby the whole way. Business Class for short haul wasn't that exciting, even for backpackers. As I was woken by the stewardess for landing, I noticed the most incredible thing I had ever seen. Yoshi's socks. If you have ever been to Japan, you may have bought a pair of these from a vending machine, but if not, I will try to enlighten you.

They looked like something your nan might have darned for a school fair or given to the local charity shop. The colour was an unmemorable mottled grey-brown, but these were not normal socks, which tend to allow all five of digits to share the same space, a kind of dorm room for your toes. No, the amazing thing about Yoshi's socks was that each toe had been afforded its own private room. Gloves for your feet – absolute genius.

They looked nice and warm, ideal for the arctic conditions you get on most flights and to prevent that awful toe sweat you get when wearing leather shoes, but I imagine it is nigh on impossible to get dressed, in a rush, hungover, in the dark, thus no use whatsoever if you needed to do a post-midnight dash back from another dorm room.

Most hostels have dorm rooms. These are roughly the same size as a normal hotel room, but they have either 6, 8 or 10 beds in them, usually bunks to 'save space'. Some have 12 or more beds and that gets a bit messy. The biggest one I stayed in was on one of Fiji's archipelago and had over 100 beds but that's a story for another time, and for the sequel to this book.

Most dorm rooms were unisex, meaning men and women, there were not that many hermaphrodites backpacking, well if there were, I didn't meet any. It was very much a family affair, and everyone got along for the most part.

The million-dollar question on entering a new dorm room was 'top or bottom bunk?' Top meant there was no chance of someone pissing their bed and it dripping down onto your sleeping bag like you were under a leaky roof, but it also meant you had to climb up, often over another sleeping backpacker, after sculling a bunch of $1 beers. The added jeopardy of falling out midway through the night heightened the anxiety! Usually, you simply took the first available bed, furthest from the door.

Given the choice, I always plumped for the bottom (insert your own jokes if you must be so smutty!). It was the ever-optimistic Casanova in me that led me to choose the bottom bunk. The risk of being pissed on was outweighed by the fact that no self-respecting woman would ever want to climb on the top bunk for five minutes of rocky, squeaky groovin' however good it was promised to be.

Come to think of it, no self-respecting woman (or for the sake of equality, man, just in case there are still any ladies who haven't already tossed this book on the fire yet, in a fit of feminist disgust) would be getting jiggy in a room full of sleeping strangers, but it didn't stop a lot of it happening. No one gave a two-hoots what other people thought of them. A great mantra for life in general – just be yourself. This isn't a personal development book, so I will crack on.

The airport was pleasant, and light, with high ceilings and latent pan pipe music that seemed to seep from the walls. The flow of people was heavy but compared to Bangkok or Denpasar seemed very orderly. Think ants versus a swarm of mosquitoes. We got into line, and soon enough, seemingly without delay, we were through customs and about to exit the airport. *"Welcome back to civilisation",* I thought. Civilisation, huh? Little did I know what Australia had to hold.

Slightly taken by surprise at the ease of our progress we stood a little gormless, looking round under the exit sign. No cacophony of noise, no hawkers pulling us into a tuk-tuk, no one trying to sell us a five-star hotel stay, diving trips with turtles, a train ticket to goodness knows where, or God forbid, a chess set. The ambient temperature was pleasant; it was all very calm.

"What shall we do?" I asked, as I thumbed through the Australia Lonely Planet (or LP as it was fondly known). Now, remember, it's Christmas 2001, which is almost the pre-internet era, and certainly well before smartphones. We needed the LP and lugged it around everywhere.

Australia, or Oz as the locals call it, is a BIG country, and I can only imagine the Lonely Planet team who create these 'travellers' bibles use some sort of ratio where the book is proportionate in size to the land mass it so wonderfully helps you navigate. The OZ LP was monolithic, the kind of thing you might use to prop a fire door open, or something a very small person might use as a stool in a busy Asian bus station. It was truly the Ayers Rock of paperbacks.

Gav looked at the book and laughed, shook his head and announced, "I am off to Maccas,"-which after a month of Asian food was certainly music to our stomachs. "I'll get the Big Macs while you read 'War and Peace'."

I couldn't really be arsed to read the '*To and From the Airport*' section so I put the book away and marvelled at the scenery out of the window. On Gav's return I confidently asserted, "Right, taxi is the best option."

We wolfed down the sweet but fatty carb-loaded junk purporting to be a burger. It tasted amazing, and just like the Fresh Prince we whistled for a cab, but when it came near, sadly, there were no dice in the mirror.

We had booked a hostel just off St Kilda Beach, which we obviously hadn't realised was all the way on the other side of the city. We were about to 'really experience' Australia. Admittedly, this 'rip-off' would partly our fault. Well, actually totally my fault.

After about 10 minutes we crossed a beautiful high, iron bridge, not Sydney Harbour quality, but the engineering was remarkable, and the turquoise blue water below was just magnificent. As we gawped out of the window, I suddenly noticed the meter was already at $20AUD; my quick maths told me it was already £7 (yes, the XE was 3AUD to £1 back then!). The city was still only just coming into view on the horizon.

I thought about asking, "Are we nearly there yet?" but didn't want to sound like my seven-year-old self, who probably had more sense than I had exhibited at that moment. I resolved to just enjoy the scenery and went back to sight-seeing. My working class self would have got out and walked.

$90 later we pulled up to a kerb in St Kilda and

jumped out, excited to get started on this leg of our journey. An Aussie hippie, working at the hostel probably for nothing more than free board and coffee, helped us lug our bags up the steps to reception; it was hard to tell if he was tanned or just dirty.

"Where have you come from, mate?" he enquired in an easy Aussie drawl.

"Bali," Gav answered.

Our helper's brow furrowed, and he scratched his forehead, pushing back his somewhat greasy mullet. "Taxi from the airport?" he asked, confused.

I wanted to say, "well we didn't swim here – our bags are still dry" but just nodded.

"Ah maaaate, youse didn't read the confo email from the hostel then." His voice rising at the end of the sentence left me unsure if this was a question or a statement. I just looked back agog and shrugged.

"Mate, there's a feckin' free bus for folks that stay here – and 90 bucks for a taxi, phhht," he didn't wait for a reply, walking away, his mullet swinging from side to side as he nearly shook his head off his shoulders.

Gav just looked at me, for once in our lives, no words were needed and it's probably just as well, given our brawl in Bangkok. We could have easily ended up having our MMA rematch in the middle of this Melbourne hostel reception.

The annoyance of being ripped off eased soon enough. It was just £30 after all and it eased even sooner for Gav as I had paid the fare and felt suitably guilty (and comparatively flush) to not dare ask him for half the money. We moved on. After all, we were in Australia.

Chapter 14 — Five Degrees and Raining? Merry 'F-ing' Christmas!

I called home around 9 p.m. Melbourne time. Mum and Dad were just about to get tucked into a fried breakfast and a Bucks Fizz before opening their gifts. I felt a bit melancholy.

Mum was excited, "Did you find the things I mentioned yesterday?"

My mum had sneaked some wrapped gifts into my backpack before we left. I had found them on day one in Thailand when I was forced to unpack the whole of my backpack just to find my favourite pair of Calvin Klein boxers. It wouldn't have been proper to meet Cambodian Royalty in some tatty Next Y-fronts!

The gifts you mean – yes – thanks Mum," I glowed with slightly fake surprise! What? Don't judge me reader, I didn't lie! She never asked when I had found them!

The questions came thick and fast, and I managed to tell no 'outright lies'. "Thailand was pretty relaxed." "The beaches in Bali are beautiful." "We haven't partied tooooooo hard." "No, I haven't found a girlfriend." "No, I haven't spent all my money." "Yes – I am looking after Gav," – well okay, that last one was a slight bending of the truth!

Then, just when I thought I was going to retain my status as the 'blue-eyed working class – boy' my mum thinks I am, she did the thing all British people do when conversation wains, she asked about the weather. I was NOT going to tell her it was 5 degrees and raining, especially when it was warmer in Barnsley than it was in Australia, so I told a big fat porky pie! Then, like a guilty child, quickly changed the subject.

Don't tell me you wouldn't have done the same thing! Summer in Melbourne is supposed to be 35 degrees, with an imminent risk of skin cancer. Nonetheless, we had had a BBQ on St Kilda beach, but the only risk to my health was the tan I had picked up in Asia being washed clean off. Or maybe frostbite.

We didn't let the weather ruin the day though. I borrowed a jumper, as I did not own a single item of clothing with sleeves, and we ate like absolute kings. Steaks pre-marinaded in some gorgeous sticky sweet and salty sauce (possibly vegemite, mate). Giant shrimps which I had only ever seen on menus before, and until that moment had assumed was an oxymoron. To me 'shrimp' meant tiny, small, miniscule but these were the size of Tyson Fury's fists. So, I now understand why you'd 'chuck another one on the barbie.'

There were burgers and snags (which you might know as sausages, or bangers, and your dog might call 'Walls'). Someone brought the obligatory green salad that no-one touched – some things are clearly a global phenomenon where BBQs are concerned. And the huge bag of Macca's fries was a magnificent addition to the best Christmas dinner I had ever eaten outside of the UK. Come to think of it, this was my first.

The sumptuous food was washed down with multiple cans of pre-mixed gin and tonic (which for some inexplicable reason didn't make it to the UK for another decade. Nowadays they are part of the daily commute for many 'Londoners') and the ubiquitous box of red wine. We pushed the boat out and got the 3l box for $10. If you were a real cheapskate, you could get 5l for the same price!

Sensing that I was losing interest with the weather conversation, Mum and Dad started to wrap up the call with the painful long goodbyes, as though we hadn't spoken for six months. We'd only been away five weeks, not to mention the fact we had spoken on the phone the night before! I wasn't disinterested in the call, I was just sobering up and needed another drink.

I had been excitedly looking forward to Boxing Day in Melbourne since deciding to leave my job some months ago. I had tickets for the Boxing Day test (that's a cricket match for the heathens and Americans reading this book!).

The only thing that could have made things better would have been if England had been in town. An Ashes test in Australia still remains un-checked on my 100 things to do before I die. And Covid has gone and scuppered my plans for 2021/2. Australia v South Africa would have to do.

The only issue was the weather – it was still cold and rainy.

Normally, on Boxing Day, 90,000+ people flock to the behemoth of a stadium known as the Melbourne Cricket Ground or for short the MCG. In the spirit of Aussie efficiency, most simply refer to it as 'The G' and almost all of them get shit-faced on mid-strength beers* whilst being slowly cooked in the sunshine.

The beer and vitamin D-induced delirium leads to the throwing of lots of blow up toys and lewd singing, but the real aim of the afternoon is attempting not to get ejected from the stadium whilst abusing the opposition players. There was also usually some cricket to watch.

The game in 2001 was decimated by the weather. It just wouldn't stop raining. It wasn't just any rain either, but the fine kind of rain that soaks you right through. We could have been in Bolton. In the end we saw less than half the scheduled day's play and the 50,000 or so who stayed at home missed the opportunity to play frostbite roulette on the frequent trips to the loo.

*2.5% alcohol, so you need to drink a lot

Chapter 15 — Casinos, Clubs and Clashes with the Locals

Whilst I didn't own anything with long sleeves, I did have a pair of smart jeans, not packed for the cold weather, but rather to ensure we could get in the 'posh' city bars. So, in our best bib and tucker, we headed off to the southern hemisphere's biggest casino.

Anything that is big in Australia is referred to as 'the southern hemisphere's biggest', although the Crown Casino no longer holds that lofty status – it's now simply Australia's biggest. Not a big gambler, I was there for the spectacle, and the fact that beers were $1. The free food that came with buying $25 of gambling chips was also a major pull factor. We headed straight for the bar.

Fed and watered, we wandered around shuffling our chips like real high rollers, but not for long. We wondered if our casino visit might well be the 'shortest the southern hemisphere' had ever seen. Surely the Aussies kept records of that kind of thing?

Gav lost his $25 in 3 rolls of the roulette wheel. So, in an attempt to drag things out a bit, I sat down at the 'stick or twist' table. I quickly learned; it's actually called '21' in Australia – they love a simplification. What? You mean it's not called 'stick or twist' here either? Pontoon you say? Isn't that a floating boat stop?

Anyway, after a couple of hands of cards, all seemed to be going well. I was starting to relax into the evening and can see why people get the 'buzz of the tables.' I still had some chips left and had won the previous hand when a 5 of clubs gave me the 21.

Then out of nowhere the Aussie guy playing next to me, dressed in sunglasses, shorts, a wife beater and thongs, angrily slammed his hand on the table and shouted directly into my face, "For fuck's sake, you Pommie cunt – if you don't fuck off from the table, I will punch your fucking lights out."

Taken aback, I had no idea what I had done wrong until someone explained to me several years later that, because I was sat in the #1 seat, I should have been sticking on anything greater than 13 in an attempt to force the dealer to twist another card. This being done in the hope that he would bust and everyone on the table would win. Don't worry, twenty years on, I still don't fully understand it either. Who knew stick or twist was a team game!

Normally, I would have kicked off, but I was so shocked, and somewhat intimidated by someone who sees fit to wear shades inside, I sat transfixed. For a moment, it felt like I was in the scene in Star Wars when Han and Luke enter the bar and the band immediately stops playing and the crazy creatures all turn in unison to cast wilful glares their way.

Eventually, I stood up, stepped away from the table, the music re-started, and all the creatures carried on throwing their money away as though nothing had happened. As I went for another beer, all I could think was, "I hope his wife is away for the weekend." It was just before 9 p.m.!

Chapter 16 — Follow the Green Man

I grew up in a very small village where it was impossible to get lost. As kids, we knew every road in the village, except for that rabbit warren of an estate called 'The Royds'. It had about 300 ramshackle 1970s houses and was known locally as "Hema". It really was the arse end of the area and we dared not venture there. I digress.

Melbourne, like many modern cities is built on a grid system, but 'Melly' retains some need for a map by virtue of having kept the 'original' street names in preference to names like 5th street and 1st Avenue. It used mostly old English names honouring royalty, such as George Street and Victoria Street but more latterly the odd Aboriginal street name had become more popular. Ironic, given that the indigenous people had been living there for tens of thousands of years prior to Captain Cook landing in 1770. The more I have travelled, and not wracked with childhood fear I have found 'getting lost' in a city is the best way to explore it, often finding things you don't find in the guidebook, such as 10p beers in a Czech Working Men's club, some of the best pizza in Rome, watching cigars being rolled in Havana or playing Mahjong with the locals in Shanghai. You just have to be careful you don't end up in the 'Royds' of that particular city.

Knowing that it would be difficult to get lost in Melbourne, I left the Lonely Planet propping the dorm room door open and set off on foot. I soon developed a technique which still serves me today when exploring relatively 'safe' cities. Every block has a crossroads at each corner, and I would always cross without stopping, simply following the green man. If you haven't done so, you should try it.

Melbourne was also the first place I had visited where the pedestrian crossings had both countdown timers and beep-tones. The ever-shortening gaps between the beeps presumably alert the visually impaired to the threat of being run down by a drag-racing hoon.

Similarly, the countdown timers were probably designed to help those who couldn't hear the 'Utes'* revving their engines, waiting for their own green light. In reality, they both just acted as an opportunity for city slickers to play chicken with a two-tonne truck. How many seconds would it take you to run across eight lanes of traffic in a suit and leather-soled shoes with only your briefcase for balance? I was amazed more 'bankers' were not run down.

*The Ute is like a workman's truck but everyone in Australia seemed to own one. Probably easier to put the surfboard or the fishing tackle in the Ute than bother opening the trunk of a normal car.

Chapter 17— Semi-Naked in a National Newspaper and Proposing to a Goddess

Attending sport as a spectator in Australia is far more accessible than in the UK. Probably because the population is one third of the UK and spread across a land mass the size of Europe. Plus, the stadia are generally much bigger. The MCG, where we froze our tits off on Boxing Day, regularly welcomes over 90,000 fans whereas the biggest cricket ground in the UK is circa 30,000.

Also, the weather probably plays a part. When it's 30 degrees, it's much easier to persuade your disinterested other half to sit in the sun for six hours, watching men in white trousers rub their balls on their balls. Who wants to watch cricket in the cold and rain? Clearly not the Aussies. On Boxing Day there were more abstentions than you'd get from the Tories when voting on any kind of social reform.

Certainly, the price of tickets makes a huge difference, as illustrated on my return to Oz in 2003 when I would attend the semi-final of the Rugby World Cup between the Aussies and the All Blacks for just $1. That's also a story for another book – probably the third in the trilogy – unless this one bombs and that story will never be told, except to anyone in earshot of me in the pub.

A Rugby Union International at Twickenham costs no less than £100 per ticket, making it a thoroughly middle-class pursuit, once more bringing into question my working class status. It annoys my mum when I go to 'Twickers' twice every year.

I love sport but I am not the world's biggest tennis fan. It was the weather and cheap and easily available tickets that persuaded me to go to Albert Park to watch the Aussie Open Tennis in 2002, oh and the fact that Anna Kournikova and Martina Hingis were paired to play together in the ladies' doubles. To be fair, I had always wanted to experience the All England Club at Wimbledon, but you need to be truly middle class for that.

Giddy at the opportunity to see a real-life goddess in the flesh and with too much time on our hands, three Canadian buddies and I decided that we should spice things up. Gav had decided to stay at the hostel to try and pull Julie - the Irish bird. Fuelled by a couple of sharpeners, on a slow tram ride from St Kilda to Albert Park, we decided that we would make a statement in the stadium. So, we stopped at a chemist on the way and purchased four sticks of prostitute-red lipstick and sneaked them into the stadium.

When I say, 'sneaked them in', I am not sure what the authorities would have done with us if they had discovered the lippy on a 'bag search'. I assume many female spectators bring their lippy in without having a single nervous heart palpitation or fear of the threat of being ejected.

Jazzed that we had not yet been thwarted, we headed to the (men's) toilets to 'prepare'. The adrenaline had already kicked in and we were buzzing. Readied, we took our seats in the stands and waited.

We saw some decent tennis played and enjoyed the spectacle. It was amazing to see how fast and agile the players were and how hard they hit the ball – even the women. Whilst our minds are on gender roles and lipstick, I had better qualify that that's a joke!

The ladies' game seemed actually seemed more 'skilful' than the men's and whilst this isn't the platform to start a debate about women's sport, I do still wonder why they are paid the same prize money when the men play five sets and the women only play three.

To put this into context, I'd be upset if my colleague and teammate, Brenda fucked off home for the weekend every Wednesday after work not to be seen again until Monday, claiming she was doing the same job as me and got paid the same. That said, if Brenda achieved the same outputs as me in those three days, I'd probably be ok with pay equality and I'd probably need take good hard look at myself and get a new job. Rant over.

Finally, the last game of the day started, and we took our places about eight rows back behind the umpire's chair. Bear in mind we had been drinking all day – fortunately it was the same mid-strength lager they serve down the road at the MCG – so we were nicely relaxed and brimming with confidence rather than totally obliterated. It didn't take long for us to steal the headlines – literally.

At the end of the first game, as the players came back to their chairs preparing to change ends, the four of us stood up, started whooping and hollering (Canadians are pretty similar to the Yanks when it comes to a whoop and a holler) and whipped off our T-shirts, to reveal the letters A – N – N – A painted in huge red letters, one on each of our chests.

Hingis tapped Kournikova on the bum with her racquet and pointed up at us in the crowd. I was the second 'N' and ashen with embarrassment, in front of about 6000 other fans, and a potentially global TV audience, all now looking exactly where Anna was - directly at me.

In for a penny, in for a pound as they say, I thought it would be a great idea to declare my undying love for this living goddess and moderately successful tennis star. In my dulcet Yorkshire tones, I yelled out "Anna – I love you; will you marry me?"

As it had done in the casino, and the bar in Star Wars, time seemed to stand still, and a hush seemed to have fallen over the stadium just at the moment I boomed my proposal.

The silence was broken with laughter. I wasn't sure if the huge crowd was laughing at the tumbleweed or me, but I did take Anna's slow shaking of her head as a 'maybe' rather than a 'hard no'.

Happy with my 'Worhol-esque' 15 minutes of fame, I put my T-shirt back on and enjoyed the rest of the match. It had been a good day, and something to remember and write about in a book 20 years later.

The next day I was a bit rough around the edges, feeling slightly woozy after an entire afternoon of beers and sunshine. I was about to get the yang to Worhol's yin - 15 minutes of infamy.

Our impromptu moment of merriment (ok maybe a good litigator could argue the make-up purchase eight hours earlier to be less impromptu and more pre-meditation) had been captured in perpetuity and distributed to 20 million sports-mad Australians.

We had made the back page of several of the daily newspapers*. Maybe not quite all of Australia saw my slightly flabby moobs but the entire hostel had – I wasn't sure if I was mortified or just hung-over. It had seemed like a good idea at the time!

When I say, 'in perpetuity', that's not an exaggeration, as the image that made print that day can still be seen on the internet today. Although I have no idea why anyone would, you can actually buy the picture. Google it if you don't believe me!

No – I didn't buy it and as you may have already worked out why, I no longer have the paper clipping which I naturally kept at the time.

*Back in the days when people actually read a physical paper.

If you haven't yet worked out why I don't have the cutting, you can either keep reading or flip to the last chapter! (You already paid for the book, so I am easy either way!).Cody, Jer and I had had to persuade Justin to come with us, by way of bribing him with beers and a free ticket, otherwise we would have been only three and thus not able to pull off the A N N A stunt. Oddly he paid for his own lipstick.

Justin took great pride in being the first 'A' and was glad he came along to share in our 'fame'. With only two friends and one bribe-able acquaintance, I am certainly less popular than the group of 10 mates who copied us some months later by spelling out Anna's surname K O U R N I K O V A on their chests.

They may have more friends, but we had novelty and these lads were on the back row cheap seats, whereas I had looked into Anna's eyes as I spoke my love for her. I am also certain that none of them ever married Anna. I never did get a definitive answer from my beau. I should follow up really – I bet she's still hot and I still have my moobs!

Chapter 18 — A Near Heart Attack on the F1 Track

Having seen my own chub in the newspaper, I decided it was time to get back into shape. The only thing that I had exercised regularly in the previous couple of months was my drinking elbow. What better way to see some of Melbourne than go for a run.

Suburban Melbourne is full of luscious green spaces and masses of Aussies who love being outside, which, makes the huge obesity problems they have in Australia today all the more difficult to fathom. They have a plethora of beautiful beaches, bays and what seems like hundreds of miles of promenades, or what the Aussies call the 'esplanades'.

When I asked someone called Bruce about why they used the word 'esplanade', he intelligently informed me, "Yeah mate, you bloody Poms tried to make us use one of your words and we didn't want that. So, we made up our own word."

Australia has at times been famous for its terrible lack of understanding of any pre-Captain Cook history so, if only claiming a French word for their own had been the gravest re-writing of the past, then we could all rest easy.

I didn't bother trying to explain to Brucey boy that both words originate from French. Promenade is some Gallic-nonsensery about yomping around the countryside while an esplanade is a flat space. I much prefer promenade.

As well as simplification, the Australian way is also to abbreviate absolutely everything and lump a 'Y' sound on the end of it. Australian becomes Aussie, Melbourne becomes 'Melly' and esplanade becomes 'espy', which also happens to be the name of one of the best bars in the whole of Victoria, and fortunately enough, within walking distance from our hostel.

As I am sure you have worked out, The Espy is simplistically named due to its position just on the correct side of the sea wall. $1 beers, a youthful, eclectic, fashionable crowd and live music from some of the best bands around created a brilliant atmosphere had brought it to promenade, I mean prominence!

I was 'lucky' to see the Proclaimers live at The Espy some 20 years after they were last famous in Scotland (I don't think they were ever famous in England). The ginger twins were still going strong down-under in 2001. A quick google search tells me they are still at it. 40 years of walking 500 miles and 500 more. They must be knackered.

The first time I went in to The Espy, I was heading down to the actual esplanade to go for my first run. I checked out a potential route from a seated position in the beer garden that first day, but I did eventually manage to leave some shoe rubber on the footpaths of the city. I was clearly committed to busting the flab.

Never being one for doing more work than absolutely necessary, I told another backpacker my plan was to use my running to facilitate the lifestyle and ensure I didn't have too much of a dad bod to get laid.

An experienced short-cutter himself, he heartily recommended I go to the organic shop (in 2001 I had never heard of such a thing) and pick up an amino acid tablet called L-Carnitine which would help promote fat loss. Also not being one for doing too much research on a subject, I took his word for it and purchased the pills. The recommended dose was 1 tablet, thirty minutes before exercise. I was intending to be out for a proper run, so I popped two to make sure I got the hit.

My plan was to run around the Formula 1 Track. Melbourne boasts a wonderful street circuit, half of which is the main trunk road into the city, but the other half is inside its city-park, and, whilst it is a public road, there's never much traffic outside F1 weekend.

It provides some beautiful scenery for a jog; similar to Central Park in Manhattan in that it has an incredible city scape on one side but boasts a beach the other. The ambient 25 degrees (at 9 a.m.) makes is a very pleasant place to work out. The feeling of having run along some of the same corners the super-charged F1 drivers would be blasting around, just a few weeks later, was quite something.

All was going well for about the first 5 km. I hit the 30 min mark shortly after and as I did, I could feel my muscles 'heating up' from the inside, like I had never felt before. A few years earlier, I had 'almost' become a professional footballer, so I was used to extreme exercise, but this was a unique feeling, to me at least. I put it down to the weather and carried on. I was halfway around, so I didn't have a lot of choice. A couple of kilometres later I was really struggling but not wanting to 'fail', I ploughed on.

Then, two kilometres from 'home' – I had to stop. No heart monitors in those days, I did the self-test to see if the ticker was about to explode. I timed 30 seconds as I counted 10...20...30...70, 80, 90, 92, 94, 96, 99. I was relieved for just a second as reconciled that 99bpm is pretty low. I had forgotten that my count was for thirty seconds, which meant my heart rate was about to blast through the 200 mark – I was only jogging, this wasn't a good sign!

My legs had turned to jelly, and I felt faint. I did my best to retain consciousness and get moving again. I did not want to sit in the glaring sun for too long, neither did I want to be embarrassed and ridiculed as some 'soft Pommie bastard' if I sat there huffing and puffing. So, I got to my feet and walked on.

The longer I was out there, the hotter it was getting. I went through hell, hoping not to have a heart attack for the next 20 minutes, before collapsing into my dorm bed and passing out from exhaustion. Another good reason to choose the bottom bunk! I woke up mid-afternoon with a hell of a headache but suffered no lasting side effects. I decided though, that running was too risky in such a hot country, so called it a day and flushed the pills!

Chapter 19 — Cricketing Heroes and a Failed Breathalyser Test

Later in January, I was back at the MCG and this time it was sunny. I was with Tom, who would be the driver of the van on the fateful day some months later, and a couple of Kiwi friends, including one of the hottest chicks we met anywhere in the world, Kiwi Emma. Or as she called herself, "Imma". It promised to be a fun evening and again, Gav chose to miss it.

He wasn't much of a cricket fan and besides, Julie, the Irish bird was staying in again. Gav had missed his 15 minutes of tennis fame by doing exactly the same thing a few days prior. He got totally blown out then and had even less chance second time around, but God loves a trier!

It had been about 40 degrees Celsius (104 Fahrenheit) in the middle of the day, so the 90,000 other spectators and I were glad this was an evening match which would end under floodlights. It also happened to be a decisive game in the 'Tri-series' (between Australia – New Zealand – South Africa) which had been highly contested, despite no-one seeming to care about the trophy itself.

The beer was still weak, but flowed nicely, the crowd raucous and the match was such that no blow-up toys were needed to entertain the patrons. Australia looked dead and buried in the game after New Zealand set a big total and the Aussies lost early wickets.

Unheralded as a batsman, Andy Bichel remained not out along with Michael Bevan, who struck one of the best One Day Innings of all time. It was truly a privilege to see some of my sporting heroes slug it out in such an epic game.

Melbourne is known for being a super hip city and the Chapel Street area has one of the best bar scenes in the World – according to the Aussies. If you frequented the wine bars and funky drinking dens, it was similarly expensive to London and attracted Australia's glitterati (well the ones that don't live in Sydney – which is most of them).

Naturally, our Kiwi friends were gutted that their team had stolen defeat from the jaws of victory. So, our post-game commiserations took us to Chapel Street, but we thought it prudent to head to a popular (cheap) backpacker bar named 'Frostbites'. It was famous for selling what we might know as 'Slush-Puppies' (frozen soda) at one tenth of the price of most bars on the street charge for a beer. They looked like the brightly coloured frozen drinks which you might buy in a gas station or at Ikea, but these were massively alcoholic. The bar had creatively called them 'Frosts'- classic Aussie simplification in action!

Where a normal bar would have had a top shelf of hard spirits, Frostbites had 23 unique, fluorescent, highly potent 'Frosts'. Each of the drums rotated in unison as they stirred the contents to prevent them becoming ice pops. It was hypnotic, and immediately set off a challenge in Tom's mind, *"Let's drink them all"*.

We started by ordering the first five Frosts - each. They were served in a half pint glass, and it was rumoured that each one contained a double shot of whatever spirit it was advertised to have. They were alcoholic for sure, but after we finished the first five in about 10 minutes flat and had nothing more than an ice cream headache to show for it, we concluded they were not as potent as suggested. Undeterred, we ploughed on. Somewhere around 18 Frosts in, we started to feel a little drunk.

As we ordered the last four frosts in the row, we were absolutely amazed to be joined in the bar by some famous faces. It was none other than some of the cricketers we had watched play a couple of hours before. Several of the New Zealand and Australian players were even joined by the South Africans, who hadn't even been playing that day. The fierce rivalry had been left on the pitch and they were now out at the cheapest bar on the strip, looking for bargain booze!

They were recognised by most of the people in the bar but were just left to enjoy their evening, which was brilliant, especially when they chose to stand right next to us at the bar. As the evening progressed, I mingled with some of my heroes: Jonty Rhodes, Baz McCullum and Dan Vertori to name drop just a few.

Initially, I am sure it was Imma that attracted them over, but after we got chatting about cricket and backpacking and they were highly amused by our 'Arctic Adventure'! We couldn't persuade any of them to drink the Frosts though. As the athletes that they were, they stuck to the beers; the last of them rolled out of the bar sometime around 1 a.m. Tom and I had finished the entire line of frosts and started to make our way back down the line. We were pretty buzzed at that stage.

Around that time, Australia had a really dangerous culture of drink-driving, and the authorities were rightly doing whatever they could to prevent and discourage pissheads from getting behind the wheel. There were adverts everywhere, TV, radio, billboards (no, not on Facebook – it hadn't been invented yet). There were 'booze buses' which was a less threatening way to describe 'road-blocks' where every driver would be stopped and tested. I was about to have my first experience of a breathalyser.

Before you put this book down and take to Twitter to try and cancel me, you can relax. I wasn't driving. I wasn't even in a car. One of the initiatives had been to install static test machines in bars and hotels so drivers could test themselves, presumably before booking a cab! As you can well imagine, it was rarely used by drivers, but frequently used by patrons looking to see just how battered they were.

We paid our $2 and had a go. I managed to blow 4 times the legal driving limit. Tom, who was a little more slender, was almost 5 times the drink-drive limit. The machine very sensibly advised him not to drive for about 72 hours! We booked that cab.

Chapter 20 — Almost Becoming a Drug Dealer

The weed in Australia was nothing like Little Gav had ever seen before, certainly nothing like the little lump of resin that he had risked his life to 'smuggle' into Turkey. He enjoyed a smoke and I'd happily have a toot (but didn't inhale –disclaimer on the off-chance I ever run for POTUS, which I believe my British nationality precludes me from anyway).

We had met four Canadian lads who would become lifelong friends. George, Neville, Peter and Ron. Ron had a dalliance or two with some of the local ladies, but turned out to be gay, which was not a surprise, and didn't make us love him any less. What was a bigger surprise was reconnecting with him on Facebook a few years ago, to see that he was now married with kids. I thought I was indecisive!

After our time in Oz, I would later visit these lads in their hometown, where I almost killed myself after momentarily passing out on a grassy patch at the back of the car park of their local bar. I had succumbed to a volatile mix of jetlag and way too many bottles of Coors*. I was safely tucked away from all the cars, so what's the problem, I hear you ask? I was clad only in a shirt and it was minus 11 Celsius.

*Canadian Beer – there are a lot of explaining the names of beers, I notice!

George, Neville and Peter were highly skilled ice hockey players and had come to Oz to do some travelling, before trying to secure contracts for the Australian Professional Ice Hockey League. Who knew that this even existed? For a country where 99% of the land mass never gets below zero, it seemed incongruous.

I thought they were taking the piss at first but alas they were not. Whilst the APHIL (or whatever acronym they decided to call it) was beckoning in the distance, for the next few months at least they were going to enjoy themselves. This included drinking, mainly Jack Daniels and Coke or something similar in copious quantity, at all times of the day or night, seemingly without effect on balance. I guess, if you can twirl around a frozen lake on a 3 mm razor blade, then a few JDs won't send you to the floor. I can't say the same for their cognition though!! Whilst their drinking was impressive, it was their smoking habits that made me really sit up and take note. They even made the Scandis we had met in Bali look like serious amateurs.

One day, a huge bag of cannabis buds arrived at the hostel. We were all sat around playing 'shithead', a very simple card game with almost no international rule variations, which made it a popular backpacker 'sport'. It was a great way to get to know people without falling out over the rules. Maybe governments should start their conferences with a few games, to get them in the mood before negotiating treaties, peace accords and such like.

Neville handed his cards to someone else, to focus on the newly arrived sack of weed. It was so pungent it could have made the sniffer dogs at Tullamarine Airport twitch, even though we were some 30 miles down the road in St Kilda. I just hoped the wind was blowing in the right direction.

Neville proceeded to split the bag into smaller bags, and, when one of the Swedes wandered into the courtyard, probably alerted by the aroma, to enquire if he may possibly exchange several of his regally-adorned sheets of plastic paper for a small sample of the green, Neville explained to him that this bag was for personal consumption. All Henrik could roll was his eyes.

I enquired quietly about the cost of the big bag and how many smaller bags could be made from the bigger bag. I did some basic maths (or math if you prefer) and quickly realised that $200 for the big bag could quite easily be turned into more than $700 by simply dividing the whole into smaller parts.

I immediately got very excited, and my business head took over. More than 300% profit and still enough for a couple of spare bifters for us. I worked out that I could travel like an absolute king, 'sorting out' a captive audience of lazy backpackers. It would be like shelling peas. However, it took less than one cycle of passing the dutchie to the left hand side to realise that this business already had a name – it was known globally as "drug dealing". I took a puff and passed, and passed on the business opportunity too. I still use this as a metaphor in my business lectures when I am trying to explain the concept to 'creating value'. Oddly, it seems to resonate rather effectively, but then half the class falls asleep and the other half head off to the vending machine for crisps.

Chapter 21 — Near Death Experience 2 (The Giant Spider)

'Dangerous wildlife' is always a concern for travellers when they head to Australia. Especially for us Brits, where the most dangerous thing we usually encounter is the 'greater spotted Stella monster' which can be seen in most Northern towns after dark, and is commonly spotted hunting its prey on a Friday. If handled with some care, it is unlikely to inflict serious damage.

There are plenty of things that can actually kill you in Oz, and you don't even need to piss them off.

Some are truly beastly like the salt-water crocodile which attacks almost unseen, striking from the riverbank like a silent assassin. It drags you under the water, rolls you round until you drown. It then leaves you, wedged under a submerged tree root, and comes back to eat you later when decomposition has tenderised your meat somewhat. It's such an efficient machine, it hasn't needed to evolve in the last 100,000+ years.

The other feared apex predator is the great white shark. Most people's fear of sharks can be attributed to the 1980s Hollywood classic 'Jaws'. And, whilst you probably should be scared of a great white if you ever encountered one, you ought not lose too much sleep. You are statistically more likely to be killed by lightning whilst golfing than you are by a shark. I was not prepared to give up golf or surfing, so just accepted the risk.

I had heard several other 'reassuring facts' used to 'encourage' foreigners to enjoy the ocean. This included the notion that sharks 'don't like the taste of human meat'. I found that reassuring, until the same surf master who told me this also explained the reason that they attack humans is that from below, a surfboard with arms and feet paddling over the sides looks rather like a seal, which it will devour like a student eating a curry after five pints.

I am not sure how you feel about this, but I would prefer not to have a massive bite taken out of me before the confused seal hunter decides I am his version of Vegemite and not Marmite. No one wants to be Vegemite where a shark is concerned (or Marmite, come to think of it). I did consider putting a sign on the bottom of my board saying, 'I am not a seal', but wondered how many Aussies could even read it, let alone their sharks. I never saw or heard of a shark attack at any local beaches whilst I was in Australia, but did religiously follow one local surfer's advice.

When me and two fellow 'wannabe surf dudes' were discussing the risk, he interjected nonchalantly, "No worries, fellas, when you're surfing, just never be the furthest guy from the beach."

I suppose it's a similar adage as you don't have to be able to run faster than a cheetah, you just need to run faster than your mate. These both make the top 10 in my list of 'Machiavellian Principles to Live By'.

There are, of course, snakes. The sly, slippery killers that, for the most part are shy retiring predators who would only bite you if you stood on one's head. Rattlesnakes, however, are territorial and will attack humans and most other animals if you have the audacity to trespass.

I did see a rattler that had made its home in one part of a children's petting zoo. Fortunately, this one was starting to decompose in the hot sun, neatly chopped into two identical halves by a spade-wielding Koala handler the day prior. You will be pleased to know that 'no children were harmed in the making of this book'.

Three of the five most venomous snakes in the world are indigenous to Australia, but they don't consider you to be a meal. If you leave them alone, they pretty much let you be too, which is why it's so unusual for a local to kill a snake. But the parents in that particular zoo were very grateful. I wonder if they teach 'spade wielding' as an elective in the Zoology degrees down-under.

Of course, there are also the spiders. Whilst snakes are shy, and crocs and sharks live in the water, so you can choose to stay away, these hideous eight-legged creatures tend to hang around in similar places to humans. The potentially terminal, venom-wielding funnel-web frequents lofts, sheds and broom cupboards. And whilst the city dwelling Redback is not much larger than your big toenail, it's extremely dangerous, so much so that without emergency treatment it can kill you.

So, when leaving the house, it's always advisable to make sure that no critters have bunked down in your Reebok Pumps or your Nike Air Jordans before you put them on.

Another great advert for thongs (flip flops in case you forgot already, come on, keep up). Also, best not go rummaging around in the loft or the shed in the dark – but I wouldn't do that, even in England.

I may have mentioned that most animals are harmless unless you do something to provoke them but, unless I was having a particularly violent spider-crushing dream, my encounter with one of Australia's goggle-eyed killers somewhat disproves my own rule.

I woke one morning to find a red lump on my upper leg. It was slightly swollen but not painful to the touch, maybe a little itchy but not of a major concern. Bed bugs, I wondered. I hoped not. Notably, it was within an inch of my left testicle. This simultaneously left me both relieved and a little disturbed. To be very frank, it wasn't even clear I had been bitten, so I did what every idiotic backpacker would do, changed my pants and carried on.

A couple of days later, the lump started to get a bit sore. It was smaller than before but had turned black and blue. I maintained it was a mozzie bite or maybe even a reaction to the soap powder I had pinched from the launderette the previous week, but my concern was starting to grow, so much so that I sought the advice of one of the female travellers, Lisa.

In the middle of the well-populated common room, I shamelessly whipped my Boardies down and pulled up the leg of my boxers to reveal the offending area to show the lucky young lady. Lisa shrieked, like she had seen an alien wearing a tutu. If only I had shown her the main man, I might have understood the outburst! I asked her if she was sure she was Scottish and not a closet American, her yelp was that dramatic.

Hearing the squeal, the others in the common room all looked over, aghast. I had my back to the room, so it was unclear (and atypical) that I had boxers on under my Boardies and tried not to obsess on the fact that everyone in the room probably assumed I was some kind of flasher.

Her advice was unequivocal. "Go and see a doctor!" she shouted breathlessly.

I looked round once more at the gawping crowd and thought about explaining, but quickly thought better of it and let the tumbleweed drift on by. I almost called this chapter *"A flasher in need of penicillin"*, but thought that might put me on a register if the authorities got wind.

I trotted off, ignoring the disgusted stares, to get my ID and insurance docs and head down to the quack's. I was 100% sure it wasn't an STD and after today, I wasn't about to get the chance to catch one in this hostel.

In the doctor's I was shown to a private room, which I was naturally pleased about, and a beautiful woman walked in. I got a little bit over-excited and started to whip off my Boardies to show her my mystery injury, and, before you could say "Quicksilver", she stopped me in my tracks.

"Sorry," she said, far from apologetically, "I left my cardigan in here."

The doctor turned out to be a middle-aged Indian English guy, which, on reflection, was less likely to end in embarrassment for me than if the forgetful female patient had fiddled around with my inner thigh.

After some prodding and poking, followed by a rebuke for not coming the day I had found the 'lump', he asked me casually if I had any idea what had caused it.

Seeing the horror in my eyes, and picking up on my need to be put out of my misery, metaphorically speaking, he cut in. "It's nothing to be worried about," he said, in a deadpan manner. This reassured me. He then continued, "You've been bitten by a spider," which *un-reassured* me. After what seemed like an eternity, he added, "You are totally fine – relax." I began to breathe again.

He proceeded to pull out a 30cm ruler. The freezing cold metal pushed against my inner thigh, causing a sharp intake of breath and a swift, involuntary contraction of my left testicle. "Three mm," he said. No, he wasn't measuring my manhood, he was measuring the gap between the now visible fang marks.

Stoically, he continued to explain that I had been bitten, unnoticed, in my sleep, an inch from my left bollock, by a 'killer spider which, based on its a 'fang size', was probably about the size of my hand.

Fortunately for me, the scarily named Huntsman spider is only a killer if you are a small animal such as a house mouse, which the doctor explained is about the size of one of the Crown Casino poker chips. I quickly calculated that would be very similar in size, but not in shape, to my left nut. Had I not been wearing my boxers, the killer arachnid could have ended my chances of becoming a dad. There but for the grace of God, and all that.

You might be wondering why I was wearing boxers, after earlier explaining that they are not part of the 'uniform'. Truth be told, I have been known to sleepwalk, as I would do on a yacht a couple of months after the spider bite, with almost disastrous consequences.

For a somnambulist, it makes my usual practice of sleeping in the nude a dangerous one in a multi-bed, unisex dorm. So, I simply put boxer shorts on, instead of taking them off at night. Everything was upside down in Australia. It is just as well really; they probably saved my left ball. Boxering-up was a practice I would continue most nights, especially after this, as half the hostel already thought I was a STD-riddled flasher; seeing me wandering around the place starkers could have tipped them over the edge.

Chapter 22 — Falling in Love with 'Bertha'

I embraced my inner hippie, which had to that point been very deeply buried. Come to think of it, I had never seen it before. It was coming towards the end of January 2002, almost two months since leaving the UK, my feet were getting itchy and city life was making a small dent in my inherited bank balance. It was time to get on the road. It was time to invest.

One of the things I loved about travelling life was the community feel. When backpackers got to the end of their journey, they would simply sell everything they didn't want. Noticeboards were a great place to buy/sell and share things such as used socks, walking boots, and tents. Who bought used socks? That still troubles me. They were also used to find people to share experiences with, no not like a lonely hearts column, things like a sightseeing trip a cheap/free ride to the next place in someone else's vehicle*

There were special sections for vehicles for sale. Cars, vans, Utes and more. It was rumoured that some of them had been owned by more than 20 different travellers, all of whom had made a small profit or broken even at the point of selling on their trusty steed.

Prices, it seemed, didn't go down, even with thousands of

Our parents might have known it as hitch-hiking. It was not one of my Mum's prohibited activities.

extra miles on the clock.* This is not an economic state of affairs the automotive industry would have allowed, if it had been on any larger scale, but for backpackers with a bit of money** it made financial sense to have your own vehicle to get you from points A – B. The added bonus was that, under your own steam, you could also enjoy choosing your own route along the way. For me it was not about economics, it was about freedom. Gav and I were ready, it was time to buy our ride. There seemed to be two options. It was either a station wagon (estate car for us Brits) or a campervan. I wouldn't be seen dead driving a Ute. I had loved camping as a kid and a campervan would be ideal for random stops in little places, and as Gav pointed out, we'd save the cost of the hostel. Most importantly, our surfboards, which we had lugged all the way from Bali, could go neatly on the roof.

We narrowed it down to two VW Campers, and although the same price, one was in much better nick than the other. The romantic in me plumped for the 1977 model, built in the same year as me. Unfortunately, that one was not in as good shape as her 1980 sibling. Fortunately for me, I was a little less dishevelled than the '77 van. Maybe there was a bit of hippie hidden deep in me all this time.

Odometer for the North Americans – I am with you on this. A clock tells time – I get it, but don't be so angry. After all, it is called English for a reason.

**flash-packers, or as my mum would say, middle–class folks*

'Bertha' was a 'puke-yellow' colour, faded after 24 years in the sun, with a white roof and as scarred as the boy at school who couldn't help scratching his chicken pox. Inside was not much better. The cupboards didn't even look clean enough to store tinned food. The fluffy purple seat in back was matted in places and threadbare in others. It just about pulled flat to become the bed and there were no curtains. The sliding side door wouldn't open from the inside without some serious brute force, which wasn't a problem today, but would become a major issue some 25,000 km further down the road.

I handed over the $1500 (£800) and I fell in love like a proud first-time father. It was mine!!!* I jumped in. Gav got in the passenger seat, along for the ride, at least I wouldn't need to advertise on the notice boards; I had my very own hitchhiker! He was already starting to run out of money and was thinking about getting work. He was keen to get to Sydney and so was I. We were off.

I had one last thing to do in Victoria before heading to New South Wales. Drive the Great Ocean Road.

The GOR, standard Ozzie Abbr., is one of the world's most iconic drives. Built post-war as a government-backed labour project to stimulate economic growth, it has been, and will be for many years to come,

*I had after all, paid for the whole thing.

the gift that keeps on giving. It hugs the coast as it meanders its way from Bells Beach, a few kilometres outside Melbourne towards Adelaide.

Bells Beach was made famous by the film Point Break where the bank-robbing Bhodi (Patrick Swayze) meets justice, while riding a massive wave in preference to being captured by the cops. Sadly, the day we lugged our surfboards down the 200 steps to follow in Bodhi's footsteps, there wasn't enough swell to drown a Star Wars figure.

Rising and falling like a roller coaster, the Great Ocean Road is a magnet for bikers, sports and classic car enthusiasts and backpackers alike. It also attracts the hoons, in their 5 litre Utes, when they are not at downtown lights drag racing and running over the bankers or the blind and elderly.

I would return, 18 months later to that same road and repeat the journey in a beautiful blue convertible and thoroughly enjoy the drive (a story for the final part of the trilogy) but for now, we were in Bertha and she approached the task at a more sedate pace on the straights. It was always a relief that we made it round the tight bends and over the steep hills. It was more coaxing than driving.

Gav had not wanted to spend the money on the Great Ocean Road trip, so planned to stay in Melbourne and get some ad-hoc work. I agreed to not forget him on my way back for the trip to Sydney.

Not wanting to go alone, I had advertised on the notice board for a 'female companion'. What did you expect! Chris had been enthusiastic to join me, although was at pains to point out she wasn't looking for a hook-up trip so I shouldn't get any ideas! Cunning plan thwarted. Christine, as she insisted on being called, presumably thought the familiarity of being called 'Chris' would be some kind of autosuggestion of an opportunity to partake in campervan erotica.

Chris-tine was American. Whilst I didn't like Americans*, I had never met a bad one. She liked rules and she had plenty. As she laid down the boundaries of non-engagement, my mind idled. Maybe she wasn't a Chris, and Christine was just her name. Maybe she just identified as Chris on public holidays or at swingers' clubs, who knew.

I let the rules slide, as she was extremely good-looking. Tall with dark wavy hair and a really athletic body, so I could see why she had set the boundaries early. She was a bit intense, but we got along fine.

I was sure that we could enjoy the sea air together and take few pictures of each other standing in front of the sandstone cliffs, which thousands of years of tides had carved into the ninth wonder of the modern world. It would only be two or three days. What could go wrong. When Gav learned that Christine was coming, his thoughts of work waned. I understood where he was

*it's a joke!

coming from. If he'd been off on a road trip with a beautiful woman, cleaning up sick and piss off the bathroom floor of a backpacker bar, or sticking my hand into a snake-infested grapevine for 15 hours in the burning sun, I would have thought twice about work!

This was the first time Gav would borrow money from me, and to be fair, I was happy to lend it to him. I was 'lucky' to have my inheritance to fall back on and I didn't want my best mate to miss out. The £1200 he brought with him had lasted less than two months. We had 10 months and at least four more countries left on our trip. I realised that it was likely that I would be bankrolling him some more in the weeks to come.

He didn't want to be 'third wheel', so he rounded up the Canadians and the five of them crammed into their station wagon, tossed their bags into Bertha and we were off. I was glad they had all decided that Christine was too 'straight' to travel with, and they'd have more fun in the car. It meant we could talk about something other than sports, getting shit-faced and shagging birds whilst farting, nose-picking and punching each other on the arm.

Some adult conversation was just what I needed. For the first hour it was fine, but I got bored quickly, and to be fair, so did she. We just didn't have much in common. We enjoyed the views. The silence was actually quite nice, but I did wonder what banter I was missing out on in the car.

I didn't have to wait long to catch up on what I had missed, as we stopped at one of the numerous lookouts and viewing points along the way. The boys would giggle and banter with Christine, which she absolutely hated. I could see the humour but was somewhat stuck in the middle.

I was committed to driving with her, but the boys were having a lot of fun, mainly at her expense, and it got to the point where at each stop, she would refuse to be anywhere near me or any of the other five. It was somewhat awkward, and I have to admit I felt a tad guilty.

Because the boys were in the station wagon, I had abandoned the idea of camping, so we aimed for hostels at the end of each day. The first night, the hostel was in a small town, just off the highway. Christine booked a single room, which drew further ridicule from the boys and turned the chilly atmosphere of the day before into an arctic frost the following morning.

At the first lookout point on day two, we were the only people there. Up early, we earned our reward, we had the view of the iconic Twelve Apostles to ourselves. Hardly a word had been spoken as Bertha chugged along since breakfast, and the view further took our breath away.

As had been the pattern the day before, I hopped out of Bertha and joined the boys. We dicked around and took some photos and although Christine might not have believed us, we were equally inspired as our more stoic and ponderous friend.

Christine stood alone eyeing the magnificent monoliths, my stomach knotted up as empathy and compassion kicked in, she had no-one to help her record this magical moment.* I reached out with the metaphorical olive branch, offering to take some photos with her in them. She offered back a slightly embarrassed, "Thank you". We shared a warm, albeit brief, smile. The ice had been broken.

The Twelve Apostles is an awe-inspiring collection of eight sandstone stacks protruding from the magnificent Southern Ocean. Christine reliably informed me that four of the Apostles had already succumbed to watery graves. I was midway through wondering if she would succumb to my charms that evening, when she spoke, unexpectedly dragging me out of my reverie.

"Penny for your thoughts," she said, obviously seeing I had drifted into fantasy land.

I quickly decided against '*truth being the best policy*', and we both laughed when I said, "I was just wondering why they had they not simply changed the name to Eight Apostles after the last one fell." Irony not being one of her strong points, and lying not being one of mine, I left it there for Christine to assume I was some kind of religious neanderthal. Bertha had been the senate for a Thatcher and Gorbachev-esque thaw in relations. Whilst

In 2001, cameras had one lens and one view finder and people had not yet learned to point them at themselves. To take a selfie, risked dropping the whole hunk of kit.

the Cold War may have been over, the cold weather was not.

At the end of the ocean-hugging highway, we had headed inland and climbed into Grampians National Park, a mountainous region close to the border of Victoria and South Australia where, after a proposed hike, we would begin the return journey to Melly the next day.

We pulled into our 'digs' for the night and once again, we were the only patrons. The huts were pretty rustic and the cold draught seeped in through the cracks in the walls. The owner cheerily informed us that despite it being summer, at night it was one of the coldest places in the southern hemisphere. There was no Google to fact-check him, but as soon as the sun set it became pretty chilly; none of us had much cold weather gear, except of course for Christine!

The owner showed us a hut for six which would be cost-effective and with six beds clustered close to each other, the likelihood of catching pneumonia was reduced. But, whilst our Cold War was over, the warm hand of friendship had not extended to the rest of the lads. So, rather than all bunk in together, Christine decided she wanted an early night and would sleep in another hut, which the lads seemed happy about. When she then expressed her fear of sleeping there alone, the lads goaded me into agreeing to staying with them to play cards, leaving her to fight her fears alone.

I let my imagination wander; were her fears a ruse to get to spend time with me? Was she setting up some elaborate courtship that would end in us making love all night like a pair of Roman Gods? Was she planning on letting me sleep, before slitting my throat and drinking my blood? I returned to thinking with my head. It was a pretty spooky place.

Cold, windy and extremely dark. No other residents for miles. One bogan Aussie keeping the dingoes at bay (at least we didn't have any babies with us). No-one wants to die, alone, in a place where no-one can hear your screams. I agreed to sleep in her hut.

Having missed out on the banter all day, I was not going to 'get an early night', but I did chivalrously walk her across to the smaller hut. Having dropped my bag on the much smaller second bed and helped her settle in a little, I made for the door. I said I'd be back after playing a few hands of poker.

As I was leaving, she expressed a further fear that she "may be cold". Specifically, adding that her "sleeping bag was not very warm". I nonchalantly offered her the use of my sleeping bag, as I skipped out of the door, ready for a beer. As I was leaving, I thought I heard her add, "Thanks, don't leave me here alone too long." Maybe it was the whispering wind.

After an hour or so of poker, a bottle of whiskey appeared, and after a couple of social nips, the drinking games began. To much consternation, I passed and left them to it. In vain, I tried to explain that I had to drive tomorrow and didn't want a massive hangover. They knew this was a lie, teasing me as I left. I had never been brilliant at reading the signals from the fairer sex, but the rye had given me a slight buzz, removing some self-doubt and providing a cause for optimism. I planned what I might say, on the off chance that Christine was awake.

My excitement dissipated quickly when I noticed that there was no light coming from the hut. Before stepping in, I pressed my ear to the door. Nothing. As I entered the hut, I remembered I had offered her my sleeping bag and my heart sank of the thoughts of a cold night ahead.

I was not surprised that she had taken me up on the offer of the sleeping bag. The surprise was that she was sleeping in my bag, on 'my' bed, which was much smaller than hers and also right next to the door.

I assessed the situation, again, thinking with my head, and, in an attempt not to wake her I crept towards the vacant bed, squinting through the dark. She had left me her sleeping bag, but it looked more like a mosquito net than something to protect from the potential frostbite.

Before I could think about just how cold it could get, a warm hand reached out and gently touched my knee as I walked past.

"It will be warmer in here," came a soft voice from the dark.

As bad as I was at reading signs, I wasn't missing this one, and as my eyes adjusted, in a dreamlike state looked down to see a naked 'Venus', barely visible in the dark. I was happy to be Mars for one night. Neither of us were cold, in case you were wondering.

Chapter 23 — Arriving in Sydney in a Cloud of Black Smoke

We readied Bertha for the epic 2000 km trip ahead by simply filling the tank with fuel. We may have pumped the tyres, but I am not certain. We were on the road to Sydney.

We would split the journey into two days and had advertised for anyone wanting a 'free-ride' as far as Canberra. We would overnight in the capital of Australia, which by all accounts had little to hold our attention, so we planned to head straight on to Sydney the next day.

Canberra was given the honour of capital, as it is loosely half-way between Sydney and Melbourne, so when the two mega-cities couldn't decide where to have their seat of government, the compromise was to dump it on the sleepy back-water of Canberra. Famously, in Australia anyway, Prime Minister John Howard, would refuse to live in Canberra, instead commuting daily from Sydney at huge expense to the taxpayer.

We had attracted a young Canadian lady, called Julie. She was keen to get to the capital but was happy to see a few sights on the way, which was a pre-requisite. I wanted to make the most of the journey and not just dash from city to city, especially after the eventual success of the Great Ocean Road trip.

We dived off the highway not long out of Melbourne and cut across to Wilsons Promontory, which when you look at the map is indeed in exactly the opposite direction to where we were going. It was only 50 km extra on the journey. It was well worth it and turned out to be 'the most southerly point' of mainland Australia, and of course a sign proudly advertised the fact. The weirdest compass based signed I ever saw was at the Cape of Good Hope in South Africa. Famous in its own right it didn't really need the huge sign announcing the most 'South-Westerly point in Africa'. Maybe the sign-planner was an Aussie.

Wild and windy and not a sunbathers' beach, 'the prom' was stunning in its beauty; we didn't see another soul. I sat on the beach just letting the world go by, watching the odd bird fly and flutter in the wind, whilst absorbing the wild scenery. Lost in my own thoughts, I felt the sense of solitude and connection with the earth run through me. I had probably only been there five minutes, but I turned to see Gav and Julie were already loitering by Bertha.

Slightly sooner then maybe I had intended, we were back on the road. I enthused about the prom, which seemed to meet a muted response. Julie was in the back, staring blankly out of the window at the wild headland. I didn't let the silence stop me; marvelling about the windswept beauty and the fact we had the entire place to ourselves, it seemed to wake Gav up.

"Yeah mate," he mused, "When you said promontory, I was thinking like a pier, you know, with dodgems, a Ferris Wheel and candyfloss."

"Prom-en-ade," I responded, incredulously.

"Uh," he grunted. I just left it there. No-one spoke until we were back on the highway.

We trundled through lots of small Aussie towns, which all seemed the same, and progress was slow. I hadn't expected the 'highway' to have traffic lights and school zones enforcing a 20mph speed limit.

Julie was pretty much mute in the back and Gav was happy to play DJ with the magic minidisc player. We stopped for a late lunch and consulted the map. We were not going to get to Canberra before nightfall. Dusk and after dark are not great times to be driving in Australia. There is every chance that you will not only see kangaroos, but you could hit one as you drive. Whilst I would never want to harm an animal, it was more preservation of Bertha that swayed my desire to drive in daylight hours. Growing to 2m tall and weighing up to 66kg, the damage hitting one at 50mph would do was unthinkable.

I asked for input from the others. They just shrugged. Despite their indifference to offering opinions, they were both somewhat disgruntled that we were going to 'camp' in Cann River. From there we would divert northwest and drive the remaining 290km to Canberra the following day. It was indeed a much bigger country than we had imagined. Outside the city, there seemed to be hardly any people.

We found a lovely little spot in the middle of Cann River, well I thought it was lovely, I couldn't tell what the other two thought. The 'town'* consisted of five houses and a general store, so the campsite wasn't hard to find. It was beautiful, nestled just off the road amongst some very, very tall pine trees and right next to the river. Apart from the owner of the site, again, we were the only ones there. It was perfect for me. I didn't worry too much about Gav and Julie.

The van slept two, at a push, so we set up the tent and got the BBQ going. There was no restaurant in 'town', so it was our only option. We had plenty of food and just as I started cooking, we were joined by a host of impromptu visitors.

Sadly, they were not a bunch of locals looking to share our fire and create a Woodstock-esque love-in. The bites we got were not ones of love and it became a race to cook and eat our dinner before we were eaten alive by the swarm of mozzies. Repellent immediately went on the list of things we needed to buy at the store the next morning, second item on the list was After Bite.

We were up early after a night in the van, well Julie had been in the van.

Out of chivalry, I had opted for the tent, as, without a

*I can only imagine the Aussie penchant for simplification means that five houses earn 'town' status by virtue of the word 'village' not being part of the vernacular.

mattress, it would have been a bit rude to make Julie sleep out there, especially as we were getting her to her destination a day later than promised. The fact that she was travelling for free seemed to be beside the point. The early morning sun had basically steamed me and Gav out of the tent. He had had to share with me – Julie was having none of his advances. The sun also meant the mozzies were long gone, probably sleeping off their over-indulgence on our blood.

Pockmarked and thoroughly slathered in Tiger Balm, but undeterred, we hit the road. Bertha smelled like a cross between your nan's boudoir and a rugby changing room. The windows stayed down, and we completed the equivalent of London to Liverpool on a single straight road, passing through three — just three — towns and saw one gas station. It was a good job we filled up in Cann River.

Our Lonely Planet informed us that Canberra was a 'vibrant student town with a thriving professional community'. We knew it would be much smaller than Melbourne, but we were looking forward getting back to civilisation after two days of hardly seeing a soul. As we approached Canberra centre, the roads seemed eerily quiet.

There were more lanes than there were cars. I looked at Gav and he looked back. "Maybe it's school holidays," he offered. I just shrugged.

"Are we back in 'Carrrn River?" he quipped.

We pissed ourselves laughing. Another ghost town. It was 3 p.m. on a Wednesday, in the capital of the country. It was just us and the tumbleweed.

Still giggling, Gav added, "We probably won't need the three days that the LP recommends!"

To be fair, Canberra was well set up. Lovely architecture, a modern city, but not a grand capital like Washington DC, London, Rio De Janeiro*, Bangkok or Tokyo. There wasn't much to see, aside from a couple of very informative museums where we did learn some of Australia's very short history. They didn't have much to say about the pre-Cook times (in the place we went to).

We left to see what was so brilliant about Sydney shortly after lunch the next day. 24 hours had been enough. Julie stayed in Canberra. If she was waiting for another traveller to give her a lift to Sydney she might still be waiting there, she seemed to prefer being alone anyway. We bade her farewell and got in the van.

The scenery changed quickly, as we headed northeast towards the coast and Sydney. Lots of rolling hills, vast rolling hills, really big steep vast rolling hills, fucking long, big steep, vast, rolling hils. The pines of Victoria were replaced by seemingly endless eucalyptus forests.

*Yeah, I know, Rio isn't the capital of Brazil, but I wonder if you Googled to check before you got to the footnote!?

We didn't see any koalas*, despite going slowly enough up some of the hills that we had every chance to look.Bertha seemed to be struggling in the heat. The gears were grinding and there was the occasional plume of smoke coming out of the engine area, which I had to inform Gav was actually at the back of the van! I knew nothing about engines or cars either, but given the driving position in the VW Camper, I wondered where he thought the engine could fit up front. We stopped to investigate the grinding and grab a pie.

The pie is the ubiquitous 'snack' in Australia and often is the only thing available at a servo**. In the UK pies come in precisely three flavours, only two of which are edible. I mean, who wants kidney-added steak? That's just wrong. The Aussies, though, had gone to town on the flavourings, which seemed infinite. My personal favourites being 'sweet chilli minced beef' or 'steak and cheese'. The latter had huge lumps of steak with a blob of molten yellow goo (like a melted craft cheese slice) just under the pastry. If you didn't get first-degree burns from the liquid cheese, it was delicious.

I swilled several mouthfuls of Bundeberg ginger beer in an attempt to prevent any blistering after too eagerly stuffing

*A koala is well camouflaged and sleeps 23 hours a day, which makes them incredibly difficult to spot in the wild. Not seeing a wild one is one of my biggest disappointments of the whole trip.

**Classic Aussie simplification of "service station", or "gas station" for our American readers!

my mouth full of pie, whilst simultaneously checking out the engine. Gav was examining the front of the van, gingerly nibbling the crust whilst blowing hard to try and cool the filling. The look on Gav's face was somewhere between awestruck and dumbstruck!

He hollered to me, "I see why the engine's in the back now."

With no mechanic to help, I diagnosed (prayed) that the issues were not serious, and we set off for the last push into the 'Big City'. We were aiming for the suburb of Manley, so would skirt the city and cross the world-famous Sydney Harbour Bridge onto the North Shore.

As we undulated our way into Sydney, the traffic began to thicken, and our anticipation grew into almost unbridled excitement. People. We pumped the music up, bobbing our heads to the beat. The single lane highway branched out into multilane suburban roads. There were people everywhere. It was refreshing. We happily merged into the flow of other traffic and looked around like little kids, smiling and waving at the locals.

They smiled and waved and gesticulated back at us, there was lots of laughter and pointing. We assumed they were just happy to see some ancestral faces. I know the Aussies tend to come across as superior to us Poms, but I had always assumed it was in faux-reverence to the Motherland. By the time I left for New Zealand, I had changed my view!

Suburbia soon gave way to the built-up city fringes, and we were looking out at town houses and industrial type buildings. The traffic got heavier still, and the smiles and waves continued to greet us at every red light. At one set of lights, Gav mused about his love for the city and people. To him, it meant lots of bars to drink in and lots of women to look at. I didn't quite understand his fascination with too much choice. A bar with one woman would be too much for Gav, he'd likely get shit-faced, fall asleep, and the juke box would have more chance of getting laid.

He also noted how 'smoggy' Sydney seemed to be. As we waited for a green signal, I took in the slightly smoky surround. I am by no means a tree hugger, but I had heard how green and environmentally friendly Sydney was. I was a touch surprised and disappointed. As we got closer to the city, the traffic became denser and so did the smog.

Ever-observant Gav noted there was no smog further down the road. In fact, the smog was very localised. Specifically, around us. We were not on fire, yet, but what would later turn out to be 'just an oil leak' was creating plumes of black smoke at the back of the van.

We immediately realised a couple of things. First, we needed to make sure we didn't break down, as that would just be an embarrassment and second it would delay Gav getting on the pull. We realised the gesticulation from the locals, which we had interpreted as intercontinental love, turned out to have been just another opportunity to laugh at the stupid singlet-wearing Poms' misfortunes.

Despite a few moments of squeaky-bum-inducing panic we made it to Manley without blowing the thing up. We duly headed to the pub for a sharpener.

Chapter 24 — Boards, Babes, Booze and a Secret 'bab Shop

Manley is a very cool suburb of Sydney. You get the beach, the laid-back lifestyle and funky locals. Situated on the North Shore, you can be in the CBD (Aussie speak for Central Business District) in about 45 minutes. But not by car, as the traffic is horrific. You have two options, an underground train or a ferryboat ride.

If you have absolutely have to commute, the schlep from the North Shore 'burbs to the city has to be one of the most pleasant on earth, and includes an incredible view of the rugged coastline that Captain Cook chose to make his gateway some 200 years ago. He was probably not sightseeing though. As the city nears, you get incredible views of the Botanical Gardens and Harbour Bridge. Pulling into Darling Harbour beside the Sydney Opera House is something very special. Why anyone choses the subterranean option, I will never know.

We chose Manley as our first stop for its fabled surf beach. A long thin strip of sand is adorned by beautiful palm trees and a wonderful promenade (yes, an Esplanade to the locals but 100% not a promontory). The waves crash in like clockwork. I felt ready for Manley, even though I had barely stood up on the one-foot waves in Bali*. If nothing else, I was confident. We unstrapped the boards from Bertha's roof and headed to the beach.

*The water in Victoria was bloody freezing, so surfing was not even considered.

142

What I hadn't planned for was the 'rip'. For the non-surfers amongst us (myself included), a rip tide is the undercurrent which pulls the water situated closest to the shore back into the ocean. The incoming wave breaks over the water being sucked back out to sea. Or something like that! Unfortunately for me, and many other folks who head into the ocean, at certain points along every beach the rip often pulls the water to the side, rather than straight back into the ocean. Uncorrected, the resulting effect is you end up drifting; at best, laterally along the beach and at worst, pulled straight out to sea.

Adjusting your position to get out of a rip is not as easy as it sounds. The tide can pull very hard. To help yourself, you need to a) realise you are in a rip and b) be strong enough to effect change. Sadly, many people have been swept away to their deaths by rip tides.

And although I don't count this as one of my near-death experiences,* being caught in the Manley rip certainly made me respect the power of the ocean even more.

Fortunately for me, I noticed quite quickly that I was in a rip. It was not my special knowledge of the sea that alerted me, but the realisation that I was suddenly 'surfing' alone, in the 'swimming zone'**. I should not be there with my surfboard.

*Maybe I should change the title of the book to '25 Ways to Almost Die Before You Are 25.

**An area of the beach/sea that is reserved exclusively for swimmers.

After some fearsome (and fearful) paddling, I did apply my limited knowledge and with cramp beginning to set in I allowed myself to drift with the tide rather than swim against it, all the while attempting to paddle to shore, and safety. After some time, and huge effort, I got closer to shore but I was paddling my board through all the horrified swimmers – a massive taboo.

As I got into the shallow waves I stood up, tucking my board under my arm, relieved that the sea wasn't going to take my life that day, but wondered immediately if the angry-faced lifeguards running towards me might render my fight with nature in vain. I stepped onto the dry sand at exactly the same time as they got to me, but, before they were able to strangle me for surfing in the swimming zone, I collapsed from exhaustion.

Their attitudes immediately changed to one of assistance rather than accusation. Anger turned to concern. It was more of a 'footballer' than a 'rugby player's' exhaustion, and with a few kind words from the yellow-and-red-clad lifesavers, I was back on my feet. Chastened and somewhat embarrassed, I dragged my board back to the surfing section. I had ended up at least 200m further down the beach than when I entered the water. Respect the power of the ocean. I laid the board on the beach and slumped beside it and enjoyed the sun and the illusion I was a 'surf-dude'.

We moved on to Bondi Beach, south of the city and not only another surfing Mecca but also a gigantic magnet for backpackers. Much like Blackpool but with a decent beach, good weather, healthy and friendly people and some classy restaurants. So not really like Blackpool at all. We reconnected with Tom, who said he had been working on an Adelaide tennis camp for a month since we saw him in Melbourne.

My favourite restaurant in Bondi, and possibly all of Australia, turned out to be a very secretive affair. The first time I went there I was a little inebriated. When I tried to tell Tom and Gav about it, they thought I was mad.

"After the bar, I got the best kebab and chips I have ever tasted, they used real meat and put the chips inside the pitta. The sauce was sensational," my mouth watering as I explained. "It's just a few doors along from the Bondi hotel," I enthused. "You know, right in between the surf shop and that fancy boutique." They both looked at me, then at one another, totally confused.

They knew exactly where I was talking about but were adamant that there was indeed nothing between those two stores.

Second guessing myself now - "Maybe next door one way or the other?" I offered.

Was my hazy memory playing tricks on me? Heads were shaken all round and they either thought I was making it up or I was so pissed I had been in Bondi Junction not Bondi Beach. I was adamant. "Come out tonight, I will show you. If I am wrong, I will buy the beers all night." It wouldn't be the first time I had been adamant about something and been wrong, so I was, needless to say, a little on edge.

By the time we approached Bondi Beach esplanade (promenade!), my nerves were gone, and I was buzzing; ready to prove myself and drink for free. We walked along the seafront and got to the block where I thought the kebab shop was. It was not there.

Ashen-faced, I dragged them to the next block of shops and then the next. Nothing. Defeated, we entered the Bondi hotel in silence. I went to the bar. It was going to be an expensive evening. Sometime around midnight, at my behest, in an attempt to keep a reasonable limit on the bill, I decided we would call it a night.

I was very quiet as we walked back towards the hostel, hoping Tom and Gav weren't hungry. They took the piss out of me mercilessly as we approached the 'ghost kebab shop'. Had I really dreamed it? I could still taste the chilli sauce that morning, so I assumed I had not.

They ribbed me some more when we got to the fancy boutique.

"Let's get a kabob," Gav laughed.

"Ooh I am hungry, if only there were a restaurant near here," they taunted.

I tried to ignore them and kept walking, just as Tom started banging on the window. Getting carried away, he started shouting after me as I hurried away, "I WANT A

KEBAB – SOMEONE FEED ME!" They fell around laughing.

Suddenly a 'door' opened. It looked from the outside like the topless/headless model, adorned with a vastly over-priced crocheted skirt and a gaudy handbag looked for a moment like it had come alive

Then, before I could say, "mad as a Parisian box of frogs", a man's head popped out and in a gruff Australian accent, he hissed, "Keep the fucking noise down, get yourselves in here if you wanna eat." We saluted the headless model and stepped into a fully-functioning restaurant.

The five or six others in the queue looked at us agog. When our turn came, the server greeted us. "Welcome to Tardis Kebabs – what can I get you?"*

*The reason for this was later explained to me as something to do with 'front-line' retail units need to close by 10pm on Bondi Beach. Genius way around the law – a secret kebab shop!

Chapter 25 — Losing Gav... For Good

Sydney was good for Gav, there was not so much nature to contend with and certainly no tents. Plenty of bars and babes to chase after, and he achieved more success than I had imagined, exhibiting persistence akin to that of Thomas Eddison. It was not so good for my bank balance, as I was now pretty much bankrolling his trip. He would later work for me, in the company I set up after travelling and pay back every penny he owed. He once drove from South Yorkshire to Inverness and back in less than 24 hours to pay for Australia! Legend.

Gav was well suited to hostel life, although he did occasionally sleep in the van, which was parked on the street in front of the hostel to save a few dollars. These dollars could then be reappropriated towards boxed wine. I am not sure I would have got much sleep in the van in Bondi. The handbrake was far from fantastic, coupled with the fact we were parked at the top of a big hill at the southern end of the bay. Should the handbrake fail, you'd be on Bondi Beach in about 3 seconds flat.

He did work but only occasionally, partly through his own laziness to get out of bed when the hostel-wide tannoy system called out for day labourers and partly because there wasn't much work that would have enabled him to save enough to carry on travelling. I felt for him.

We had lots of good times together in Sydney, but one day he came to me with a glum look on his face and announced, "I can't keep borrowing cash off you for the next year, I am going to get a job."

"Ok, mate, what you gonna do?" I enquired.

He then shocked me with his curt response, "Fruit picking."

Don't get me wrong, being paid to spend all day outside, pulling apples off a tree or grapes off a vine, whilst getting paid a decent bung, free board and food sounds cushy enough. Until you remember you are in Australia.

The sun is 45 degrees in the middle of the day, the ozone layer offers no protection and if you don't get skin cancer or dehydrate like a sultana, killer snakes and spiders inhabit the fruit trees. Add to that the digs were 20+ people to a room, with no air-con. Many had no windows. Add to that, most farms are a shit-ton of miles from anywhere, and it's not a rosy a proposition. In fact, some backpackers have reported mental health issues from extended periods of Granny Smith-flavoured toil.

So, off he trotted to Bundaberg. There was no pomp and no ceremony. I went to the station at Bondi Junction with him and said "Adieu". We would meet up in a couple of months when he had saved enough to carry on travelling. 'Bundy' is a hick town, a couple of hours' drive north of Sydney, made famous by its ginger beer and infamous by a backpacker who purportedly threw herself off a bridge right in the middle of town, plunging to her death.

Some weeks later I got an email from him, asking for a bung. He explained that he had not been able to save as much as he had hoped. After long boring days in the fields, the long boring nights were too much. A card school had stripped him of some of his earnings, and the Bottle'O* had deprived him of even more. He spent 10 weeks in a vicious cycle of 12 hours avoiding cancer and vicious animals and 12 hours of drinking and playing cards in an attempt to forget about the days.

My ire began to rise as I read. How could he need more money from me? Why couldn't he have the discipline to save? I jumped ahead in my mind, told myself I would refuse point blank to lend him anything else. Blood pressure rising, I read on. Just like the lifeguards in Manley, my anger soon turned to empathy and concern.

In addition to the boredom, which I considered to be the price of the freedom he was trying to pay for, he had gotten some kind of bug which had laid him up for about five days. He explained he was very weak and bedridden. If you didn't work, the farm owner took your money for the privilege of staying there. If you had no money, he gave you credit.

*A Bottle'O is what we might call the off-licence, or liquor store. Although in Oz, they are often massive drive-through warehouses where the server chucks slabs of beer and cases of wine onto the back of your Ute. You rarely pop in for just a bottle of red to go with the impromptu Bolognese. This one delivered, both booze and weed!

It was seven days on, seven days on! No SSP (Statutory Sick Pay) when you are fruit picking, and no union to protect you. He added that he had probably returned to the fields too soon and was about to get sick again. He had saved a little, but not enough to make it worthwhile and he needed to get out. He agreed to borrow £500 from his mum, but dare not ask her for more. £500 wasn't enough to get home. Home? Home to England. My stomach sank; his trip was just about over. I called him immediately and we discussed what he needed; I transferred the cash.

To add salt into his very fruity wounds, it struck me as extremely harsh that he couldn't change his ticket to get back to London by flying west. He had to keep going east. He confirmed his remaining five flights (Melbourne to Auckland; Auckland to Fiji; Fiji to LA to Vancouver, and Vancouver to Heathrow).

He would spend the minimum of time (and money) in each of these amazing places simply to get home. It would take him almost 10 days and the best part of £1000 in additional expenses! Ouch. The final ignominy was that his mum would drive the four hours from Barnsley to pick him up in London. I can't imagine the conversation flowed much on the drive up the M1.

Chapter 26 — "Doing Time" in Gaol (Jail)

With Gav working in Bundaberg, I decided to settle down for a while and moved Bertha and my stuff up to Bondi Junction. It was a small bungalow with two rooms. Two Irish sisters occupied the other room and I was bunking down with a crazy Jewish kid from Devon called Jamal. He was like Ben Shapiro on speed – he even rabbited away in his sleep.

I looked for a job. One of the sisters said her employer wanted extra help. She was working in sales and was earning good money on a 'commission only' marketing 'thing' as she loosely described it. I decided I didn't have the skills or the 'attributes' to persuade pissed and horny men into a 'titty bar'* and as good as the perks may have looked, I left her to it.

Her sister worked in 'construction'. It turned out that she went round with a bunch of Aussie road diggers as they repaired busted water pipes. She got the dubious honour of being one of the two 'Stop/Go' operators and spent all day manually instructing cars to either wait or proceed, simply by turning her pole.

*Titty bars are pretty common across Australia (well, they were in 2002). They are actually called titty bars! And if the name doesn't explain what they are, it's simple. The female bartenders wear nothing above the waist except for a smile.

I learned that the other pole spinner was a 6ft Swedish sweetheart from Stockholm called Stella. I didn't think they'd be hiring me, even if it was a three-way stop! I am sure the pole spinning girls took some frightful sexist abuse from the bogan Aussie workmen. But at least they didn't have to dance around their poles, and it was surely safer than fruit-picking. The added bonus for her was that if there was so much as a vague sniff of rain in the air, they got to go home for the day and still pick up the day's pay.

Unable to find a sensible job, I got desperate and ended up in gaol*. Just to be clear, I wasn't incarcerated! I had applied to an agency, and they asked if I would interview for an 'admin job'. It was becoming clear that job titles were pretty vague down under. I interviewed at an office in the CBD and met someone from the staff.

Betty was Head of Operations at the Long Bay Correctional Centre and she seemed keen to hire me after a very short interview. I agreed to the job and was happy with the rate of $16 per hour (£5.50 ish) tax-free. Well, I wasn't going to declare it if they didn't make me.

Betty shook my hand and welcomed me to the team. Her handshake was firm, and she held on for a moment longer than I had anticipated. Before I could escape her grasp, she added firmly, "I expect you to honour the whole three-month contract."

*Gaol is an old-fashioned version of jail. This was certainly an old-fashioned place.

I winced in pain as her grip tightened,-which she clearly took to mean a nod of agreement. It was the first I had heard about a fixed-term contract. Three months, what the…

She let go of my hand and I almost collapsed, wringing my wrist, and before I could regain my composure, she headed for the door.

"Report to the Ops Centre at 8 a.m. sharp – just tell the front gate you are here to see me," were her parting words as she disappeared through the door.

I wracked my brain (which was busy fighting the pain in my knuckles) as I tried to remember where the gate had been on the way in. There hadn't been one? Was I imagining things again? I wondered if I had misheard and resolved to turn up a bit early the next day. I was happy to have an office job and not be working outdoors.

Before I had even got on the bus back home to Bondi Junction, my brick of a mobile phone rang and it was the recruiter. The front gate Betty mentioned wasn't in the City Office. I was heading to the gaol. In Malabar. A suburb of South Sydney, situated right on the headland on some of the most expensive real estate outside the CBD. It's just a shame none of the rooms have a view. It was a further shame that the commute would take me an hour, each way.

I drove Bertha up to the front gate of the Maximum-Security Long Bay Gaol the very next day. Nervous and expecting an interrogation at the gate, I was waved through without so much as a word. Maybe they were expecting me, or thought I was someone else. It seemed a bit lax.

I parked as instructed by Gate C, which led to one of the secure wings in the 'inner sanctum' of the jail. I was ushered through the gate of what looked like a medieval castle, complete with portcullis. Security here was a little more rigorous, which was good as this was the last stop before entering into the recreation areas, where the prisoners would spend their 'non-cell' time.

The guard remained by his desk and offering only one directive as I entered for the first time, "Just don't talk to the Chesters."

I looked around, I couldn't see anyone else, he must have meant the inmates. I walked through unaccompanied. A handful of prisoners milled around, carrying out 'work tasks' for which they earned some 'chicken'*.

Betty didn't come out to meet me and I stood, uncomfortably lost, gawping around. Finally, with no-one else to help me, one of the 'Chesters' pointed me to some stairs. I nodded my thanks, cautious not to engage. I knocked on a door at the top of the stairs; three ladies looked up, clearly not expecting me. One of them waved me in.

*Chicken is money inside. Pay was less than $0.50 per hour so it was more like the amount of chicken you'd get in a bag of crisps than in a bucket of KFC.

It was unlocked. The only thing separating the staff from the inmates was an unlocked office door and 16 stairs; I counted them one day to work out the amount of time I would have to arm myself with a sharp pencil in the event of a riot. Four-seconds if you were wondering!

I would have a lot more time with my thoughts over the coming 10 weeks (yep, 10, not 12). On day one, Betty had been called into the CBD to see some government minister or other. She would not be back today, I was told. I filled in an HR form and then read a book. The girls in the office promised I would get some work to do but didn't know what to give me. Bored of the book, I picked up a blue folder.

I thumbed through the 'LBG Handbook'*, which sounded more like a sexuality guide than an HR file. Disinterested with staffing procedures or bank holiday protocols, and just about to put it back on the shelf, I stumbled on a list of names. It was an inventory of the inmates; a basic description of their crimes (murder, robbery, drug dealing, etc.) and the length of their sentences in ascending order down the page. It was pretty chilling stuff.

I had been there about six hours, I wasn't locked up (well technically I was, but critically I could choose to leave at any time) and I was already bored out of my mind.

I pondered the list and tried to imagine six weeks, six months, six years, 16 years, 26 years of being locked up

*LBG = Long Bay Gaol

for 23 hours per day; being told when to eat, sleep and shit. My head started to feel like it was about to explode. I wanted to run but decided to man up and get paid for reading a novel!

At about 4 p.m., one of the ladies offered me a cup of tea and we all sat around chatting. They finished work at 3 p.m. each day and clocked off at 4.30 p.m. They were happy to let me join in their chat, or as it turned out, suss me out.

After some frosty initial questioning, I was interrogated about my background and took great delight regaling them with some of my tamer travelling stories. The ones I have shared with you wouldn't have made a great first impression.

I concluded with my upcoming plans to visit five more countries and complete my circumnavigation of the globe. Part-fascinated and part-incredulous, they explained that they were all born in South Sydney, went to school in South Sydney and all lived within 10 minutes of the jail. Two of the three had never even left the state of New South Wales, let alone been abroad. One had been to university, at, yep, you guessed it, the University of New South Wales in Sydney.

Maybe they liked my accent, or my shirt, either way they confided in me that Betty was the 'sworn enemy' and they had initially treated me with a dose of suspicion, fearful that I may be Betty's mole. Presumably planted to bring to light their clock management indiscretions.

I assured them I was happy to toss it off 90 minutes early every day if they were. They also let me know lunch hour was a loose term to include one full clock hour. 11:30 a.m. lunch start would last until 1 p.m. If you were forced to work until, say 12:10 p.m., lunch would extend to 2 p.m. We were immediate friends.

The conversation was easy and light until I started asking questions about the 'Blue Book'. Apparently, that should not be seen by anyone without 'appropriate clearance', which none of them had, but somehow, they also knew all the contents.

It made me wonder, what due diligence the state of NSW had done to credential me for the job? Maybe they had checked with Interpol that I wasn't on the 'Red List', but I doubted that. Given my interview had been less than 24 hours prior, there had been no time to check with the UK that I didn't have a criminal record, which, in case you are wondering, I don't. I signed nothing so much as an autograph, let alone a contract, NDA or privacy agreement and still had my passport in my pocket so they could at least take a copy of my ID.

Again, security seemed a little lax. I was a foreigner, free to wander around mixing with the country's most dangerous criminals, inside a maximum-security prison. What could possibly go wrong? Undeterred by my own breach of data privacy, I ploughed on with the questioning.

I was keen to know why there were two women in the 'pen' and was surprised to learn that they were considered to be such dangers to themselves and others that 'no other facility in the country could handle them'. "Fucking Mental Psychos" was how they were described by my colleagues, which I assumed wasn't either technically or politically correct – but we were in Australia, so I went with it.

It turned out there were more than a dozen of Australia's most notorious, serving in excess of 25 years and I also learned that "L" next to a name on the list meant LIFE. "And life means life – no parole for those fucking monsters," I was sternly told. I was in no doubt there were some serious menaces to society inside the same walls. I shivered.

"Lifers are not the worst though," one of the ladies continued. "It's the Chesters that really make your skin crawl."

I replied in a questioning tone, "What, those guys I saw working on my way in they look harmless enough?"

All three of my new best friends burst into laughter. Amongst the hilarity one of them spluttered, "Ah, maaaaate, you are so naïve." I was taken aback, these yokels, never been out of the state, how dare they call me naïve?

After a moment of silence, Betty's assistant, Kylie, quiet up to this point, broke her silence by explaining,

"Chesters are sex criminals, kiddie fiddlers, violent rapists, child porn 'stars', and dads who fucked their own daughters."

I really did shiver, and these beasts were wandering around sweeping the dust and watering the plants. I thought about carrying a pre-sharpened pencil on me full time.

Not done yet, Kylie continued "The ones on the 'B' wing over there, are the fucking fag* sex pests. They are kept away from the others or they'd all be dead in a week." There really is no honour among thieves – yikes.

I settled into prison life, I mean life in the prison. Careless lips sink ships, as they say. Work was easy and often fun. I got to drive Betty into the city and sit there in the car for hours listening to Nickelback and The Proclaimers on the radio while she went to meet with 'Senor Importante', real name unknown, before giving evidence in court.

It was cushy. I actually really liked Betty – maybe it was the fact we had both been overseas (or just out of the state) but the girls in the office and the staff in the city offices all treated her with a good dose of fearful respect and openly called her a 'vicious lesbian', which I found to be a little less than respectful. We got on well.

*Slang term for homosexual which I wouldn't normally repeat but I think the guys Kylie refers to here have bigger things to worry about than the descriptors used in my book.

Occasionally, I got bored of Nickelback and wanted to remind myself I wasn't still stuck in 1995 waiting for Punxsutawney Phil to announce the end of winter - and I would wait for Betty outside the car. I'd prop myself on the hood, sweep my hair like Jonny from Greece, grab a Bundy and watch the world go by, wondering whether I should try and prove them all wrong about Betty's sexual preferences.

All was going swimmingly well at the gaol and the most exciting thing I had to deal with was being attacked by one of the local birds. No, not my colleagues, an actual feathered flying bird. It had decided to nest right in the middle of the green space between the car park and the portcullis gates.

Every day, I was forced to sprint from Bertha to the safety of the security entrance – I am certain no one else has ever run so enthusiastically into a prison before. Or since. Oddly, it seemed not to attack any of my colleagues. It could probably smell my Pommie cologne.

Aside from dodging racist seagulls, I was either driving Betty around or working four-hour days and getting paid for eight. So short of work was I one day, they set me on cleaning out the store cupboard, which was essentially a huge room where everything not in immediate use had been dumped.

I only learned about the funnel-web spiders after I had dragged out the supposed one day 'spring clean' for more than a month. I eventually got bored of being locked in a windowless cupboard (it was locked to keep the 'Chesters' out, not me in) so decided I ought to finally admit the job was finished. None of the girls ever came close to that storeroom.

Clearly this was the test and I had passed, eventually. Things were about to get interesting. The next day I was told to go and audit 'A' wing.

Whilst I was slightly unnerved at doing my work with rapists wandering around unsupervised, I wasn't particularly scared. As one of my female colleagues put it in her inimitable Aussie way, "You are unlikely to be their type, mate."

I am not sure how the three women I worked with felt about the situation of their office. It was like the zebras setting up home in the middle of a pride of Lions. I was sure that Betty would have been able to handle the lot of them on her own if anything had kicked off.

'A' wing audit complete – I was sent to 'B'wing. And, if you were paying attention earlier, yes, this is where the homosexuals convicted of sex crimes were housed. To me, 'B'wing had always been a Star Wars fighter ship, but this was different, and I was pretty much shitting myself. Sphincter almost uncontrollably winking.

I was in my early 20s, wearing a floral short-sleeved shirt and a pair of skinny jeans with flip flops. My boyish good looks*, sun bleached quiff, brilliant blue eyes and long

*If I do say so myself, and probably shouldn't.

162

eyelashes, which were probably visible from the other end of the shower block, made me prime meat.

I was moderately reassured to find that whilst the audit was to take place, all the inmates would be in their cells. I clenched my jaw (and my bum cheeks) and went in. Twenty minutes later I was done. I had a list of serial numbers, including one from the condom machine, which had been situated conveniently at the entry to the communal showers. I suppose you don't want homosexual paedophiles spreading HIV when they are finally released. Parts of this world are seriously fucked up.

It seemed I hadn't turned a single head. Not sure whether to be disappointed or relieved, I knew one thing, I was glad to be heading back to be with the straight rapists realising I would never enjoy Star Wars again.

The following day I was sent to do more audits in different areas of the gaol. Most of the inmates were in their cells. When I entered the Supermax 1 unit, the head screw casually noted, "The cons are on free roam, mate – you ok with that?"

"Yeah sure," I replied, not really knowing what he had said (probably a language thing).

"You want some company?" he followed up. Not wanting to sound like a soft Pommie bastard, I politely informed him I would be okay, thanks.

"You can talk to them if you want, just don't go in the cells," he added, almost postscript as I was halfway out of the door. *Don't go in the cells?* I wondered to myself.

The kitchen audit was fine. I wasn't attacked with boiling water or garrotted by the toaster wire. In fact, the 'crims' were genuinely affable. Some small talk ensued. They were mainly fascinated by my ending up in the slammer halfway around the world. The guards were as relaxed as any in the whole place. It got a bit dicey as I moved onto the wing to audit the items which would take me past maybe 60 cells, all the way to the showers at the far end.

As I left the kitchen, my mind flashed to prison dramas I had seen on TV where a 'fish' enters their prison for the first time, the satanic screams and the threats seem to be scarier than spending all day locked up. In fact you'd probably choose to spend 23 hours locked up if it meant only one hour to survive.

Fortunately, there was no abuse for me, apart from a bit of raucous laughter and some piss-taking of my shirt. I wanted to shout back, "It's better than the puke-green jumpsuit that you all seem to think is fashionable round here," but I remembered at least three of these fellas were here with no chance of parole. I was here until 4:30 p.m. – if I survived. I bit my tongue.

I continued down the wing, realising that all the cell doors were open. Not unlocked, I mean wide open. The prisoners were just wandering around as they pleased. The only place in the jail that held more theoretical danger was the Supermax 2 wing next door. It was apparently necessary to ensure separation between the Aboriginals on 2, and the white supremacists that I was currently being wolf-whistled by.

I did indeed make it out alive and had only one noteworthy comment for the audit. I remarked,

> *'There seem to have been one or more serious parties on Supermax 1. With almost two weeks to go in the month, the reserve tin of tea bags is more than two thirds empty and both condom machines are flush out of rubber'.*

When you are doing 10+ on the inside, societal norms change. Who am I to judge, but I have never liked tea that much. I guess, if there's no coffee available, what you gonna do!?

I got to know some of the people in the jail quite well. I even took part in a 'screws v cons sports day' which was similar to the kind of thing that as a proud parent you might have gone to watch your 8-year-old take part in.

There was even a sack race and various relays. I assume egg and spoon was cancelled as a spoon might be deemed a weapon. Instead of a bunch of pre-pubescent boys and girls being forced to race against each other, this was hardened criminals racing against the same people who would likely spit or piss in their food if they managed to win. The paedophiles watched on, from inside their cells, salivating (I assume at the imagery of a children's sports day).

Curiously, the jail ran with very few staff. The perimeter guards were armed with rifles, which looked like something from Dad's Army and aside from the five of us in 'admin' and the screws, the other roles were performed by the inmates.

They mowed the grass and tended to the flowers, they mopped the floors, did the washing, sorted the mail and made the meals. They even maintained the fleet of cars which, apart from Betty's and the governor of the jail (the big boss), were all pooled Holden's Camaros.*

One Friday night, the lax security I had observed previously on my first drive in, came into sharp-ish focus. The conveniently tinted windows of the guvnor's car, which had been in for an engine tune up, allowed one brave inmate to become an outmate.

He simply drove up to the main exit boom gate, rolled the window down a couple of inches, waved his hand at the guards who promptly let him drive out into the Sydney suburbs. They had failed to notice that the governor had left for the weekend, some hours earlier in one of the pool cars.

It wasn't until the next shift that anyone noticed.

Vauxhall Astras to the Europeans reading.   To the Americans still here, it's just a very small vehicle.

I imagined the search would have been a frenzied manhunt, with the cops chasing around the city trying to catch the absconder with Thin Lizzy's 'Tonight There's Gonna Be a Jailbreak' blaring out in the background. It turned out to be a bit more sedate.

I learned that, just before lunchtime on Sunday, almost 48 hours after the 'breakout', a local police patrol alerted the gaol that they had found the guvnor's car. It transpired that the address where the vehicle was spotted, was that of the mother of the 'outmate'. He had been there all weekend.

The admin girls and I laughed when we heard that the outmate had asked the local cops, "What took you so long? I was expecting to be back in on Saturday morning." The mandatory five-year addition to his sentence seemed like an expensive price to pay for a maternal cuddle and a home-cooked meal (or four).

I learned after the second 'escape' a few weeks later that it wasn't uncommon for career crims or those who had been inside for a long time to try to break out. The 'mandatory five' would ensure that they didn't have to re-enter society. Despite the extensive reintegration work that goes on towards the end of long sentences, some offenders simply slip through the net.

Sadly, it's not just the weekend wanderers who don't get to the end of their sentences. In three months, there were several DICs, – 'Deaths in Custody'. Some from natural causes and a couple of inmates decided that life in Long Bay was just too much for them.

As far as I know they were no inmate murders in my time there, but one of the women inmates did try to shiv* four of the guards before turning the blade on herself. The report stated that enough blood had been let that day to support a small hospital. It took two more guards to overpower her and the five of them survived, albeit sliced like a loaf of bread and somewhat light-headed. The room must have looked like something from a Tarantino set afterwards.

All in all, it was an incredible experience. A very dark cross-section of society but all human beings. I was hugely grateful for Betty hiring me into Long Bay, more grateful that I was free to leave whenever I wanted. Although I thought she might lock me up when I said I didn't want to work the final two weeks of my 'contract' which had never been signed. I said after almost three months inside, I needed to leave Long Bay and go to Byron Bay and get stoned. She understood and signed my early release forms.

I thought about changing the names of the jail and the staff involved but given that I signed nothing, there is probably absolutely no record of me having worked there so they have the ultimate plausible deniability. I wondered if I had imagined the kebab shop. I knew this experience was very real indeed.

*A shiv is a homemade stabbing device usually made from a razor blade and a toothbrush handle. Not sure what she needed to shave but hey ho.

Chapter 27 — Unleashing Bertha, Backpacking Again

Gav was gone. Jamal, my crazy roomie, had also skipped town and I had served my time. Sydney had been a blast, but it was time to get on the road again. I was about to be joined from the UK, by my very attractive friend and former colleague, Becky.

The whole company thought we were having an affair when we worked together – sadly we weren't - but I didn't do anything to quash the rumours. Now, she was coming halfway around the world to drive up the East Coast of Australia with me for the next three weeks. The tongues would be wagging again, for the duration of her holiday and no doubt long after her return. The only drawback was (or was it?) that she was going to be 'chaperoned' by her older sister.

Not only did I get early release from Long Bay, I got early release from my apartment. Instead of giving six weeks' notice, I moved next door for the final two weeks ensuring the landlord (who happened to own both properties) had no 'down-time'. Win-win.

I was somewhat surprised that my temporary roomie would be a lady. "She works nights, so you will hardly see each other – I hope it's not too weird for you?" the landlord asked quizzically.

"Not at all," I said. I am not overly shy, as you already know!

It turned out that she was a stunning bottle-blonde, with stark eyebrows, not like those heinous things they are painting on their faces these days, but real black hairy ones that if you don't tame, spread like wildfire. Nicole's were proper hair, expertly tamed and framed her face beautifully.

In our brief encounters, usually her coming home and making her 'dinner' as I was having breakfast, I gleaned that she worked as a receptionist in a 'lap-dancing club,'. She mimed the quote marks and smiled; we both took that to mean a brothel.

I wanted to ask her, was she really a 'quote, unquote' receptionist? I held my thoughts and the chat remained friendly but there were no 'signs'. You will know by now, I am pretty bad at reading signs.

The couple of weeks passed quickly. I finally got the oil leak fixed on Bertha. At least we would draw less attention leaving Sydney. I added a few home comforts, including some kitchen utensils and herbs and spices to pep up the BBQed meat. I also added handmade curtains, which were just about able to block out the light from a candle. They were about as opaque as a pair of fishnet tights.

I did, however, make some good last-minute additions the day before departure, including two coolers, one for beer, one for food, and a charger. I stocked up with steak and Castlemaine XXXX* and I was just about ready for the

*Yep, another brand of beer.

off. I even packed my bag the night before, ready to pick up Becky and Rachel at 9 a.m. the following day. I hit the hay, contented with my time in Sydney and slid into dreamland excited about the journey ahead.

I dreamed of beautiful beaches, the soft warm sand between my toes, sumptuous surf crashing onto the rocks sending spray high into the air, the smells of BBQ and the sound of clinking bottles; laughter carried for miles on the warm breeze and Bertha thundering down the highway.

I dreamed of our voices singing along with Shakira, and steamy encounters with a beautiful woman sliding in bed next to me. The dreams got more vivid, almost lucid, and deep in my subconscious, I could hear a soft female voice whispering to me, but I couldn't make out what she was saying.

I mumbled my dreamy responses, desperately trying to identify this siren. As I did so, I started to become aware of the room around me. I was no longer in the van, but to my surprise it looked exactly like the room I had gone to sleep in. Indeed, it was the same room; I was dashed, no longer dreaming.

Disoriented, but I could still hear the whispering beauty. As I came to, I was delighted to find that my roommate had got into my bed after her night shift. The landlord was right, we barely saw each other; until we saw each other bare. The thought of checking if she really was a 'receptionist' seemed inappropriate, so I let that thought slide. I left Sydney very fulfilled, and I was extremely late picking Becky and her sister up.

Chapter 28 — Byron Bay Beaches and the Nimbin Cookies

Byron Bay was the heaven to Long Bay's hell. It's a hippie paradise, where anyone and everyone are welcome to come and go as they please.

Two long golden expanses of sand are watched over by a majestic lighthouse. Perfect surf breaks off the point and draws visitors from all over the world, who risk getting dumped on the rocks for the thrill of the almost never-ending barrels.* Whilst it's still technically in New South Wales, I was sure that my colleagues from the gaol had not ventured this far north of Sydney. Byron was so laid back it really should be in Queensland.

Not fancying being thrown around the on rocks like a rag doll in a tumble dryer, I left the boards well and truly strapped to the roof of Bertha and spent some quality time on the beach. I didn't need the board as a talking point. Flanked by Becky and Rachel, I was already happier than a pig in shit!

One day, when it got too hot to just sit in the sun, a partly-shaded coastal path offered a tremendous walk to the cliff head for a closer look at the lighthouse. The sea breeze took the edge off the temperature, and energised by the opportunity to see the migrating humpback whales, we

Waves which curl over but don't break. It looks like the surfer is inside a barrel.

made good progress toward the clifftop. We didn't see any whales, but we did see the sign which proudly advertised that we were now at the most easterly point on mainland Australia.

Having detoured to Wilsons Prom on day one in Bertha, I had now inadvertently been to two of the four outlying compass points on the mainland. I would have to return 18 months later to see the most westerly spot; Steep Point in the appropriately named state of Western Australia (see *More of My Road Less Travelled* if you can't work out why it's called that – or just want a laugh some more!) but the idea to get as far north as Cape York was now set in my head.

I don't think I am spoiling the book by telling you Bertha didn't get there. Neither did I, by virtue of the fact that to access Cape York you have to navigate some 400 km* of unsealed road (no tarmac or whatever you call normal road surfaces in your country) and is accessible only by a 4X4 and a hired driver.

The gloss quickly wore off that idea, so I reimagined the

At the time of publishing, almost half of the 400 km to Cape York has been sealed and the proud boast from the 'Peninsula Development Board' alerts tourists to the fact that 'As of 2019, only 200km will remain unsealed'. 200km on sealed roads might take about 3 hours of comfortable cruising; on an unsealed road, closer to 10 hours of bone-jarring, head-smashing fun – and almost certain death if you broke down. No thanks!

goal and was aiming for Cape Tribulation – the 'Most Northerly place with a Sealed Road on Mainland Australia' – I wondered if they'd have a sign to honour the fact.

I could tell you all about how I lived my best life in Byron Bay, hanging around hot surf chicks with other bronzed stallions, drinking Tooheys New* until the sun came up, riding my first barrel wave cheered on by Mick Fanning, getting hit on by Stephanie Gilmore and meeting Patrick Swayze filming Point Break 2… but none of that happened, so I won't lie! In truth, Byron Bay is as beautiful as everyone says, the beach bars and post-surf scene was good, but nothing too much happened whilst I was there. Becky, Rachel and I had a lovely time relaxing and enjoying the weather, the beers and some gorgeous tucker **.A short drive inland is a little village called Nimbin, famed among backpackers for being the only town in Australia where cannabis is legal and boy, Nimbin makes the most of that status.

I "ummed and ahhed" about going to Nimbin, which has been described as 'a social experiment' and 'an escapist subculture'. I had heard it was full of puffed-out zombies, which I didn't think was really my scene. I went along with Tom and the girls to see what it was about. It was a sleepy backwater with sweet FA going on. It certainly wasn't the 'Drug Capital of Australia' as one dissenting publication put it! Never believe what

*you guessed it, another beer.

**Food.

they write in the newspapers.

You could obviously buy weed to smoke, which became passé (the dutchie to the left hand side) – after a week in Melbourne. But you could also get cannabis cakes and cookies, charas chocolate, Mary-Jay meringues, hemp horseradish sauce, bhang butter, blow-brews, pukka pot pies, golden grass Greek salad and ganga grapefruits. I kid you not, well maybe I kid you a little, but there was cannabis in almost everything.

In fact, there were more products available than words to describe them. It was hard to buy anything which wasn't infused with drugs. Naturally the place to sit and sip your 'Draw Darjeeling' was called the 'Happy Café'. I giggled at the irony – or was it the air that made me giggle?

Apparently, Nimbin is also famous for environmental initiatives such as permaculture, sustainability and self-sufficiency, but I have no memory of that! The only thing I really enjoyed was the cinema, which was set in a beautiful old church and had a capacity of 12.

The projector was nearly new, back in 1977, and the seats were a higgledy-piggledy collection of 'previously owned' sofas, seemingly donated by local residents. It was very cool with lots of local art adorning the walls; they even served free tea and cookies at the interval, I assume to keep you chilled out enough so as not to notice the rusty springs protruding through the sofas.

It really was a great experience but in a hippie town where material possessions are actively discouraged the sofas were a major tetanus risk. Imagine how battered a sofa must have been to be rendered no longer fit for use by its zombie owners.

We headed steadily north, camping and chilling out in some amazing towns, crossing the border into Queensland, which oddly means a time-zone change. Queensland doesn't take daylight savings, meaning the clocks don't go back or forward like they do in the rest of Australia*.

Brisbane, the biggest city in Queensland is situated just across the border from NSW and many people cross the border for work. This clock-based anomaly means that for half the year, commuters who travel north lose an hour on their journey so must get up extra early. Don't worry though, they can potentially be home even before they even set off from the office. I imagine they need a trip to Nimbin just to get over the stress of that or regulate the jet lag.

*After a three-year trial in 1992, 55% of the state voted "leave" in the daylight savings time (DLS) referendum. Rumour has it that the vote was won by "leave" as they promised $100M AUD (around £40M) per day to the state coffers if DLS was left behind and this was where Boris got his 'Brexit Bus' idea from.

Chapter 29 — Jez

We had made it into Queensland. By-passing Brisbane and staying just one or two nights in each place. Rural Australia was stunning, and the few people that did inhabit the small towns (remember, no word for village in 'Australian') were absolute salt of the earth type people.

The food and fresh air was amazing, and we were even treating ourselves to expensive wines, not the boxed ones, the ones that come in an actual bottle. We didn't go over the top though, sticking to the screw-top versions, despite having a bona fide corkscrew in the van.

By the time we reached Noosa, we had said au revoir to Becky and her sister. We had been for short walks, long meandering drives and generally had a very nice time, but there's not too much to report and you don't really want to hear me describe the scenery all day.

Tom was still hanging around and we had built up a nice friendship, but a new kid was about to come onto the travelling block. Twenty years after meeting Jez, we are still best of friends today and it was at Koala's Hostel in Noosa where we first were introduced.

To be honest, I am surprised we became friends. He was a few years younger than me, probably just a bit better looking, certainly a lot thinner (he had a six-pack, and I didn't), he supported Liverpool and I am a Man City fan; he's a southern fairy and I am a tough Yorkshire bloke.

He already had two friends travelling with him and I had Tom.

We had nothing in common really and no reason to be anything other than rivals for the fair Maidens of Noosa, except; there was a five-a-side football tournament and combined we made five Brits. The smallest commonality brings people together when they travel, and us Brits have always been happy to come together against a common enemy.

International football has always been a curious thing. Fierce, and in the 80s and 90s vicious rivalries existed between British club sides but, when abroad, that was mostly forgotten in the bid to defeat the common enemy - foreigners. And if there had ever been a war between the nations, winning was a means of vengeance. How parochial!!

The International Five-A-Side competition was on. Sadly, there were no Germans in the competition, they were probably busy laying their towels on the sun loungers for the next day, but we had been drawn in a mini-group with the next best thing: a Japanese team.

After winning our first match by one goal to nil*, thinking how well we had gelled having met less than an hour before, we stepped off the pitch and got the chance to watch the Japanese team play the same opponents we had

*Nil means none – zero – nought or zip depending on where you are reading this.

just beaten (a coalition of Europeans). We were buzzing and full of nationalistic pride, observing the diminutive Asian foe we would face in 15 minutes' time.

Our buzz quickly went flat and then turned to trepidation as we watched, jaws hanging, mouths agape, at just how good the Japanese boys turned out to be. Fast and skilful, they had clearly played together before. They passed the ball beautifully in the very tight pitch, making fools of the team we had just beaten. Their main striker showed cool, sharp finishing: they won 6-0.

The pitch was small, even for a five-a-side game and surrounded by tight netting on all sides, including the 'roof'. The ball was always in play. It was 10 minutes per match, with the only break being for the change of ends at half-time, and of course fouls. The goal had not been as easy for us to find as it turned out for the Japanese.

As the dishevelled EU team crawled out of the hole in the netting, Jez got the lads into a huddle, and we quickly put together some tactics.

- They were fitter than us so we would use tactical fouls to slow the game down.
- They were more skilful than us so we would use hard fouls to stop them.
- They were faster than us, so we would use off-the-ball fouls to stop them.
- They shot better than us and we didn't have a proper keeper, so we would foul them to stop them shooting.

Not very sporting but neither was Pearl Harbour*. Would the Japanese's skilful approach and tactical brilliance enable the victory, or would our heavy-handed tactics prevail as they had in 1945?

We didn't want to beat the Japanese because they were Japanese. We just wanted to win. They were absolutely lovely lads, but in that cage, we didn't give them a chance to play. It was like five heavy-weights in an MMA bout with five fly-weights.

The tactics worked and we reduced their skill to pretty much zero. Gave them no sight of our goal and gave away 20 fouls in 10 minutes. A dubious penalty enabled Jez to score the winning goal.

Just like Hiroshima, 'we' had won, but it was hardly a triumph, and we would be knocked out ourselves in the next game.

We consoled our skinny Asian buddies, bought them a few beers for their troubles. It turned out that they were all 17-years-young and studying nearby. Three of them were representing Japan Football at junior level and had been champions of this tournament five times out of the last six they had been in.

It was a fun evening watching the competition unfold with these very cool young men and they forgave our heavy-

*I realise that Hiroshima and Nagasaki were even less sporting than Pearl Harbour but that wouldn't have given us the necessary drive to beat these boys.

handedness, and we did a fair bit to extend international relations.

The biggest success of the night was that our little friendship group had formed. Charlie, Rob, Tom, Jez and myself would not be far away from the action on the run all the way up the East Coast.

We had also seen enough to know that Jez was a good footballer. He and I discussed our football trials and tribulations experienced during our flirtations with the professional game. The more Tooheys New we had consumed, the better we had been as 16-year-olds! Jez and I had a lot in common after all. And our shared interests would grow as we headed north.

Chapter 30 — Fraser Island

Over the next few days, the talk of us playing football turned to watching it. The 2002 Football (Soccer) World Cup was about to start in Korea and Japan – on our time zone, which was a stroke of luck. We needed to plan the next couple of weeks very carefully, as we were also approaching two of the 'must-do' activities on the east coast of Australia.

Fraser Island is the biggest sand island on the planet (not just the Southern Hemisphere) and the Whit Sunday Islands provide epic sailing adventures for those who don't like sailing in the wind! The jeopardy of Fraser Island and the Whit Sundays was there would be no TV at either, hence no football.

England were scheduled to play three group matches. Drawn against Nigeria, Sweden and (one of) our arch-nemeses*, Argentina, whom we loved to hate after they invaded the British territory of the Falkland Islands in 1982, which we probably colonised from them at some point. The seemingly pointless war was fought 300 miles off the coast of Argentina, some 8000+ miles from the UK.

*When you write something like this, as a Brit, you realise that in modern memory we have been at war with, enslaved, colonised, so many nations that our list of nemeses is pretty long. Add to that the disdain we have for some of our allies and near neighbours, it's a wonder anyone likes us at all.

The two sides spent 10 weeks fighting over a boggy marshland resulting in the deaths of almost 1000 troops (from both sides), and amazingly only three local Falkland Islanders. But far more than the war, we hated Argentina because of our meeting in the World Cup four years previously, and back in 1986 when Diego Maradona punched the ball into the goal knocking us out in the quarter finals.

Shortly after half-time in the 1998 World Cup game between the two nations, Diego Simeone fell over when David Beckham petulantly aimed the flick of a heel at him. Feigning injury and rolling around on the floor in faux agony, egged on by one of my 'soon to become ex' idols, Gabrielle Batistuta, Simeone's actions led the referee to send Beckham off.

Despite a heroic rear-guard action for 43 minutes of the second half, an agonising 30 minutes of extra time ensued and with no further addition to the score, we suffered the all-too predictable English mode of defeat, losing on penalties*. Which made the whole defeat harder to swallow and our thirst for revenge even greater.

The 1998 defeat led to some gratuitous stories in the UK press, and stomach-churning scenes at football grounds across the country, which amounted to the absolute vilification of Beckham. The poor guy even had death threats sent to his family.

*Leeds stalwart and hard-man David Batty missing the critical spot kick.

It was frankly a sickening reaction and indelible stain on the sport but, incredibly, Beckham has not only recovered from this but become one of the game's global superstars – and promptly replaced Battigol (Gabriel Batistuta) as one of my heroes.

In 2002 the whole of the UK was now behind Golden Balls*. The tension had been mounting for months since the football gods pitted these two great teams together once more. First up for England though was Sweden, which would be followed four days later by the Argentina game.

Tom and I booked our trip to Fraser Island to begin a day after the Sweden clash and we would return to Hervey Bay on the morning of the Argentina match. Jez and his little crew would be on the island at the same time but in a different group to ours. We agreed to meet up on our return.

It seemed every Swede under the age of 30 had descended on Australia in 2002. They were everywhere. I assume Sweden was pretty much empty. The travelling Swedes were pretty similar to the travelling Brits, they liked a drink, they enjoyed dorm room life (trust me!) and most were easy going; always happy to share their weed and a good laugh! But maybe the key reason the youths of these two nations got on so incredibly well was that we had not been at war with Sweden (save for a short battle in 1810), and as colonial aggressors it seemed we had forgiven their Viking pillaging.

*Beckham's nickname – oh, how times had changed.

The afternoon kick-off drew close to a thousand travellers into the semi-open air bar in the middle of Hervey Bay town. The bar had probably never seen so many patrons. Faces were painted blue and yellow or white and red. It was standing room only, many people standing on tables.

Of course, there was no segregation and ultimately no animosity. I was proud to be English and proud to be a football fan that day. I can't always say that. The game was terrible, and the teams played out a cagey 1-1 draw, which was acceptable to all, but meant we would more than likely need to beat Argentina in four days' time to ensure we qualify for the round of 16.

Slightly worse for wear, I had a fitful sleep that night, oscillating between dreams of glory and nightmares of defeat to our South American foe. I woke with the more pressing thoughts of Fraser Island on my mind. I was excited to be going camping.

Tom and I met the 10 other random travellers in our group, with whom we would share a couple of 4X4 Jeeps and tents, for the next three nights, as we roamed around one of nature's true wonders. It promised to be epic.

The giant, uninhabited sand island is the biggest sand island in the world and a wonderfully wild slice of nature. We would be getting right down with that nature, as there would be no supplies once we embarked on the short barge ride from Hervey Bay. We made our introductions to our new buddies and went to the supply store.

We picked up tents, stoves, flashlights and all the other practical things and then worked out how many bangers* and burgers, beers and boxed wine we'd need for 72 hours. It was just about enough to sink the Titanic. Hopefully it wouldn't sink our barge which would whisk us across from the mainland.

The island has no roads, so we all took a lesson in driving on the wet sand, and crucially, how to get out of 'soft sand', just in case! We were expressly told not to drive on the soft sand or, too close to the sea. Any salt damage to the vehicle would result in the loss of our deposit, as would any paintwork dings, so whilst there were no cops to stop you from drink-driving, it was actively discouraged.

Tom and I looked around at our new team and spotting the one tea-totaller in the group, quickly assessed she'd be more of an asset than a pain in the arse, seconded her into our 4X4. She was designated driver for the afternoon. Tom and I promptly popped open a couple of cans and toasted a 'back-to-basics bonanza'. We would not be disappointed.

Fraser Island was wild, with much of the island un-passable, certainly with our driving skills, but there were a few 'must see' spots that gave the trip some structure.

With a plan in place, we swiftly reversed the order of all the things we would visit, to ensure that we had the least

*Sausages.

amount of driving to do on the third morning. There was no way we would miss the Argentina game, stuck on an island with no TV.

Fully ladened with beers and BBQ supplies, our 4X4s set off for the coast. We would head to the north-east coast of the island and work our way back south, which meant a long drive on the first afternoon. Tom and I sat in the back and enjoyed the scenery and the beers. The ride was bumpy, which was probably to be expected as we were thundering along the beach. We were delighted when we came across the famous Fraser Island shipwreck, not least for the opportunity to get out and stretch our legs.

The S.S. Maheno had run aground there whilst on tow to somewhere else on the east coast in 1935. The Mehano was ripped from the tug amidst a cyclone, and despite not having power, the crew managed to run the boat aground on the island, find their way ashore and set up camp, much like we were about to do. Rather than pay to remove the vessel, its New Zealand owner left it there to rot. Despite disowning the vessel, the owners did not disown the crew and came to their rescue a few days later.

Anywhere else on the coast, it would probably have been seen as an eye-sore but, here, there were no locals to complain. By 2002 it was just a rusty hull, still recognisable as a boat with a few windowless portholes. It remains a popular photo-stop today for the few lucky souls who get across to Fraser.

The iron-red rust created a wonderful contrast against the golden sand and the azure-blue water, which in turn melted into the cloudless baby-blue skies. It is actually an awesome sight, only seen by the comparative few who make the trip to Fraser Island. After we had taken our obligatory photos with heads poking through the portholes, we got back into the jeeps to head to one of the camping grounds.

The 'camping grounds' were designated by the wardens of the island, not because there were any facilities but presumably as they were relatively safe areas to camp. I.e., fires wouldn't easily spread across the entire island. I also assume consolidating the places available to camp made it easier to clear up any mess that was left, although to be fair, we didn't see any rubbish and took all of ours home as instructed. We wanted our deposits back, oh yeah, and of course to preserve this unique environment.

The first night camping was epic. On a massive high of being in the wild and still clean enough to feel human - we wouldn't shower again for at least 72 hours - we pulled into the wooded area where two other groups were already setting up camp.

A big fire was roaring, there was music coming from some tiny speakers somewhere close by and although it sounded like it was being played inside a tin can, it said one thing to me and Tom: "Party!" We got dressed up in our best 'camping night out bib and tucker'*, which

Tucker in this context means clothes, not food.

simply meant putting on a light fleece (borrowed). The evenings were chilly.

The beers and the conversations flowed. Everyone was enjoying the freedom of being in the wild. Tom was about to take 'being in the wild' to the next level. He had got chatting to an American girl who looked pretty nice. It was dark, baggy fleeces and combat pants were the standard uniform and girl's hair was tied up, caps and hats worn and the only light to check out the quality of a potential mate was the firelight – everyone looked good.

Tom's American friend wasn't much of a drinker and used this ruse to get Tom away from the fire. They headed off for a walk, hand in hand. Some twenty minutes later, Tom was back with a big smile on his face. Being the gent that he is, he would not tell us what happened in the sandy darkness. His friend hadn't come back to the fire with him, thus I assumed nothing had happened and his silence was to save him being caught in a lie.

That theory looked like it was going to be borne out very shortly afterwards, when the very same American wandered over hand-in-hand with another gentleman. Tom looked a bit gutted, and I mercilessly took the piss. "She's upgraded, buddy." "You must have been useless." "She's blown you out and moved on already." "She's going to kiss him…"

And sure enough she did, but rather than get angry and punch the guy's lights out, Tom just burst out laughing. Doubled over, hardly able to contain himself he managed to utter the incredulous words "She's not even had time to wash her mouth out." The rest of us joined the in with raucous laughter. Maybe she told her new mate that the sea was the cause of the salty kisses.

The next day, we made the tricky inland drive to Lake McKenzie and wow it was worth it. The huge freshwater lake has some of the cleanest water on the planet. Filtered millions of times by the microfine sand and unpolluted by human hand, with maybe the exception of a few backpackers passing their own water into the mix.

Surrounded by jungle, the multitude of green shades merged seamlessly into the magnificent blue water. The beach a thin sliver of pristine white sand. The water closest to the beach offers an unbelievable contrast to the blue-green depths further out.

It is like a warm bath, totally clear, fish easily visible as they dart around your legs, but if you dare to stride out just a few metres the water turns almost midnight blue. Beyond the ledge looking down at an unseeable depth immediately makes the heart quicken. For those brave enough to step into the unknown, the temperature drops as rapidly as the depth, shocking the body into involuntary shivering.

It's an intense and crazy feeling of contrast, akin to letting your bathtub go cold while you are sitting in it, and then running the hot tap hoping to warm it up. But unlike your bath, no matter how much your swirl your arms back and forth, round in circles, up and down, there is no way to mix all this water around you in Lake McKenzie. If you want to swim – it's freezing.

To warm up, all you have to do is get back into the shallows or go and lie on the beach! We dared each other to swim across the lake but everyone agreed that it would bring about certain death, so we just settled on having another beer while we discussed how far we might theoretically get before sinking!

Later, around the campfire, legendary stories of unidentified monsters lurking in the deep at Lake Mck' did the rounds, but they can't have taken any backpackers. The water was just too cold for anyone to be out there long enough to be eaten.

Aside from snakes and scorpions, which we didn't see any sign of, there was a natural predator that we were told to be aware of on the island; the dingo. Unique to Australia, Fraser Island boasts the only remaining 'pure' colony of these beautiful creatures. Closely related to wolves and the dogs we keep as pets, they are actually quite vicious and can attack humans if provoked (or hungry) but their timidity meant if you were smart they were of little concern.

Keeping food well packed away and not straying off too far from the group was about all you needed to do to protect yourself. The only real complication came when nature called. With no official toilets on the island, it was normal practice to take a shovel, hide behind a tree, dig a hole, squat, 'aim' and hope you didn't shit on your ankles, then refill the hole.

The dingo 'threat' meant we were advised to take a 'shitting-mate' with us, especially after dark. Now, I am not very sensitive about these things, but I imagine there were people who didn't take a dump for the entire three days rather than face the prospect of being watched while they squatted over a sandy throne. I dare say some travellers missed out Fraser Island altogether, so as not to have to dig their own WC.

Even for the more hardened amongst us, it wasn't a comfortable experience. It wasn't as bad as the Bangkok bus station, but imagine wandering into the pitch blackness, armed with a spade, a few sheets of 2-ply paper and your mate holding the torch, vulnerably squatting semi-naked, hoping that a dingo didn't creep out of the darkness to bite you on the arse; all the while trying to concentrate on hitting the invisible target below. As you can imagine, it was a swift, potentially frenzied experience; the Times crossword would have to wait until we got back to a hostel.

I like my home comforts as much as any man, but Fraser is a special, unspoiled, truly beautiful place where you can reconnect perfectly with your natural state. There's something truly liberating about fending for yourself and surviving. Ok, ok, we took vehicles, food and firelighters with us, but it was as self-sufficient as I wanted to be. I got the experience, so why bring on more hardship?

Being (almost) back to basics reaffirms a lot of things about life and gives you time to appreciate what you consider normality. We had had the most incredible party, among sublime nature, cooking meat and drinking beer at every meal. I loved Fraser Island.

The only reason I wanted to get back to Hervey Bay was the Argentina game; oh, and having a bed to sleep in, running water, a hot shower, some food that wasn't garnished with sand and of course three walls and a locked door around me as I contemplated that crossword.

Chapter 31 — Beckham's Redemption

After 72 hours of semi-roughing it and partying way too hard, with somewhere between little and zero sleep and no proper ablutions, we returned to Hervey Bay. The short barge ride was irksome and not much conversation ensued. We were so close to a hot shower, yet so far away.

The Eng. v Arg. match in Sapporo was drawing near and rather than being hyped up for the encounter, Tom and I wearily wondered whether we would stay awake through the game – sleep was about all we could think about. We had not been hungover on the island; when you have a beer with breakfast that tends to be the way, but the effects were kicking in now.

We checked back into the hostel, dumped our sandy backpacks in the corner of the room and just looked at each other. Fatigue seeping through us, legs heavy, eyelids drooping - desperate to close and succumb to the dreamland.

We fought the urge to lie on our bunks, encouraging each other that we'd feel better after a shower and other bullshit PMA* statements! Looking like something from Shaun of the Dead, Tom then made the ridiculous claim that the only way he could manage to make the game was to stay off the beers. I rolled my eyes and with a new energy, got in the shower.

*Positive Mental Attitude (nothing to do with menstruation, in case you were confused).

I was down in the bar first and got us a spot with the rest of the crew. The bar was jam-packed, but we had great seats in front of one of the many big screens. As the kick-off drew near, I began to wonder if Tom was going to make it. Maybe he had fallen asleep? Just before kick-off, a voice came from behind me, barely audible above the booing of the Argentine anthem, requesting a coke. I nodded and pointed Tom to the table we were watching from. I ordered a tray of Jaeger bombs (and no coke).

The atmosphere in the bar was one of a deep desire for revenge, for the apparent injustices of four years prior and 1986, for those of us who could remember it. Everyone was extra nervous. The draw against Sweden meant that in all reality, we needed a win to give us the best chance of qualifying for the next stage. A draw would be sub-optimal* and a loss meant we were out.

The pantomime villains of Batistuta and Simeone lined up, hands on hearts, belting out their patriotism; Simeone choked with emotion and almost in tears, somehow managing to scream the words of the anthem at the camera as it panned past him; Evita this was not.

The game was tense and not that memorable as a footballing spectacle. However, Beckham was heroic; running, sliding, jumping, heading, tackling and of course

*And a likely last 16 game versus Germany, who we had been good at defeating in wars but not football. Maybe if we could substitute in America at half time, we'd beat them at football too.

passing those sublime balls that only he can, frequently causing the hundreds of millions of people watching, from all nations, to collectively gasp for breath.

His desire and drive was visceral, there was no way he was going to let 1998 go unavenged and just before half time, after Michael Owen was brought down in the box, there was only one man going to step up to take the penalty.

Cue Golden Balls. Or more accurately massive balls. The pressure was intense. The entire world watching; including his own countrymen who had previously shouted death threats at him. In the past four years, he had worked so, so hard to become an absolute icon all around the world, on and off the pitch. Here he stood, risking it all again, for his country and our dream of a first World Cup trophy since 1966 resting on a knife edge. Missing was unthinkable.

Beckham placed the ball on the spot. Even he looked nervous, but he shut out the fears, the doubts and the childish sledging of Simeone and Batigol. Regaining his composure with a couple of huge deep breaths, he ran up, slammed the ball into the net, delivering the goal that handed England the victory by the narrowest of margins.

The ghost of 1998 exorcised, his redemption now entirely complete, the whole world falling in love with this real-life phoenix. Little did we know at the time, but it would also be the blow that sent Argentina crashing out of a tournament that they had been one of the favourites to win. Sapporo erupted and just like the beer which makes the Japanese city famous, Beckham's revenge had been 'served cold'.

Chapter 32 — 'She Who Must Be Obeyed'

Hervey Bay doesn't have much for backpackers to do. It's known as the gateway to Fraser Island and now an indelible memory of World Cup glory for me and everyone else in the pub that night. We hadn't won the cup, we hadn't even got past the first stage, yet this felt like the ultimate glory.

We had beaten (one of) the old foe(s) and we dared to believe that we might just be watching England in the final, somewhere further up the coast, and crowning off the entire trip with us lifting the much-coveted Jules Rimet trophy for the first time in almost 40 years. It made me giddy to think about it.

Keeping it real, Captain of Doom, Tom reminded me we still needed at least a draw against Nigeria in our final game of the group stage or it would all have been in vain. The England team had a few days rest before that and we needed to get to Airlie Beach so we could watch the game, then spend three days sailing around the Whit Sunday Islands on a famous Whitbread Round the World Race yacht.

The team would get bigger in Airlie Beach; A squad was beginning to really take shape. Tom and I arranged to stay in the same hostel as Jez, Rob and Charlie. We arrived at Koala's backpacker's hostel, and it was more like an 18-30s club than a hostel.

Koala's encapsulated the tropical feel you get as you drift further north. 'Dorm rooms' were individual wood huts, still with six or eight beds in them, but far more glamorous than the city hovels we had been used to. On site was a restaurant and a proper bar that other hostel dwellers would descend on each evening. We didn't need to venture too far from base.

Airlie Beach is a bit of a misnomer (at least in 2002); the main beach happened to be a man-made lagoon around which imported palm trees and fake grass attracted hundreds and hundreds of backpackers each day. We lounged around, blasting competing musical tastes out of micro-speakers and drinking mid-strength beers from plastic glasses. It was like being in Melbourne, but warmer! And the cricket was impromptu games with kids bats and tennis balls.

The town's popularity with backpackers is mainly centred around it being the first gateway-town to the Great Barrier Reef for travellers heading north. It's also where most of the yachts pick up guests to explore the Whit Sunday Islands; a haven for sailing enthusiasts. Stunning beaches and incredible views of the natural beauty of Australia from the sea make it a must-do event, even for those of us who have never really sailed before.

Unlike Hervey Bay, Airlie has forged its own reputation as an absolutely outstanding stop on the backpacker trail, irrespective of whether you were heading south, or, like us, drifting north. It was a place to soak up the sun, meet others and have a serious party. As you will probably have worked out by now, I had found a decent party at most of the places I'd been along the way, but this was entirely different gravy!

Jez and the boys had met up with a couple of other travellers they knew, so their hut was full. Tom and I joined four other random travellers, which was a bit of a disappointment as we'd be 'dorming' away from the growing group. Our disappointment turned to joy as soon as we entered our hut.

My jaw almost hit the floor. Stood in front of me was an absolutely stunning young woman. Long black hair, curves in all the right places and the biggest, deepest chocolate-brown eyes I had ever seen. Our eyes met and we were instantly in love. Well, not quite in love but she was damn hot.

"Ayesha," she said, by way of minimalist introduction. She daintily shook my hand and added, "It means she who must be obeyed." I quickly punched myself in the chest to get my heart going again.

'Aysh' was travelling with Amy, who was also absolutely gorgeous; a fact that wasn't lost on Tom, for whom it actually *was* love at first sight. Sadly, unrequited at the time, and repeatedly so on a multitude of future occasions. In fact, he's probably still in love with Amy. As well as being smoking hot, both Ayesha and Amy were a huge amount of fun and added some more, and always welcome, Yorkshire-ness to 'The Squad'. We had a team of 11 to support our 11 English 'heroes' in the upcoming game against Nigeria.

As England always seemed to do when expectations rose, they managed to disappoint versus Nigeria. But crucially, unlike '86, '90, '94 and '98 they did not break our hearts prematurely. A lacklustre draw saw no goals and very little in the way of inspiration. We fortunately qualified as runners-up in the group and following some other weird results in other groups would face Denmark, rather than the unknown quantity of Senegal, in the last 16.

The general consensus was that Denmark would be the easier of the two opponents. The potential jeopardy was waiting for us in the quarter final. We were odds on to meet Brazil* but first we had a few days to get ready for Denmark. We said au revoir to Airlie and hello to 'The Card'.

*Even the Argies who had been knocked out would be supporting us in that one– well maybe!

Chapter 33 — 'Sleep Sailing'

'The Card' was a sleek and stylish 60-foot sheath of bright yellow carbon fibre. Sitting pretty, bobbing up and down in the turquoise waters, we were welcomed aboard.

The Card had been built to contest the 1989-90 running of the Whitbread Round the World Yacht Race; and although it was my first time on a racing yacht, I had no frame of reference, it looked fast! Fortunately for us, the owners had refitted the once-bare shell, to become a beast, set up to cater for paying guests to sail in speedy comfort.

Including me, there were six guests on board and along with the skipper and first mate, we would crew the yacht (after some on-the-job training). The two diminutive Aussie girls, currently chopping carrots below deck, would be cooking and cleaning in the newly-appointed galley. Bunks were angled tightly against the curved hull of the boat, underneath the main deck – I grabbed a bottom bunk.

The next three days promised to be a fast, frenzied, windswept sailing heaven. Naturally we stocked up with plenty of beer and boxes of wine too.

Sadly, The Card met an untimely demise amidst high winds in 2012. After breaking free of its moorings at South Mole Island, a decade after we had moored there, she was washed onto the rocks and torn to shreds like the tissue paper that had been through the 'shit-chopper' toilet on board.

Whilst we didn't want boat-wrecking high winds, we did want some wind. It was like being in the doldrums on the first day. Even windward side of the islands barely saw a breeze. We cruised on the six-knot motor and didn't even bother to raise the sails. The upside was it was perfect sunbathing and beer-drinking weather. We made the most of it and found a cracking spot to snorkel.

We were advised always to swim and snorkel on the starboard side of the boat. Suspecting the avoidance of jellyfish or shark attacks, one of the paying crew enquired as to why. The skipper's blunt reply came, "Well, mate, if you are swimming port side when someone takes a shit, you will be eating it without even knowing."

When the on-board toilet is flushed, a suction pump with force greater than 1000-Dysons kicks in, sucking your shit away. You guess where it goes?! Yep - straight out into the sea, but only after it passes through a blender which chops your logs up into little pieces on the way out. From that moment on, we 'clung on to the starboard bow' (Jim).

Free from the worry of eating each other's faeces, we snorkelled freely, experiencing a plethora of fish, including millions of Nemos (clownfish), turtles, rays and some of the most incredible corals on the planet – who needed wind?

After we had dropped anchor for the evening, I did spot some people from another boat swimming portside. I dashed below deck, ripped a few small sheets of loo roll, stuffed them into the pan and pushed the flush button. With a slurp and a slug, similar to the noise of the dentist vacuuming spit from your mouth, The Card spat out my ghost shit and a confetti of loo roll. Childishly, I dashed on deck to see the passengers from our neighbours' boat swimming away from us, faster than if they had seen Jaws!

The next day we got the sails up and learned how to crew the boat, which was fun but hard work. I was secretly glad it wasn't windier as there'd have been a lot more to do. The bit of wind we did have meant we could get out to Whitehaven Beach, which is probably the whitest sand on the planet, or at least the southern hemisphere. It's the beach on all of the Whit Sunday postcards for a reason. We walked to the headland to get a bird's-eye view, almost tripping over a snake along the way. The sunset was sublime, and it is one of nature's most unspoiled places. We were truly blessed.

As darkness fell, we enjoyed a BBQ on the beach before using the skiff* to get back on board. Everyone was sun-kissed and shattered. The sea and the salt air have an amazing ability to leave you feeling totally exhausted but also incredibly relaxed.

A guitar appeared and we merrily sang songs and sipped our drinks; the increasingly inky sky was awash with twinkling stars.

*Small blow-up boat.

After an idyllic day, the tiredness took hold, and we prepared our bivouacs on deck – the bunks below looked too small and sleeping under the stars was way more romantic. One by one we dropped off into a deep satisfied sleep.

"Hey, mate, what are ya doin'. Mate. MAAAAAATE!" Apparently, I was the last person in the Whit Sundays, and maybe all of Queensland to hear the frantic shouting. I looked around and oddly, I was the only one on my feet. I saw the rest of the boat looking up at me aghast.

I was at the bow, leaning right up against the 5 mm wire ropes that ensure you are not washed away if you fall overboard; when clipped on. I was not clipped on and said rope could not have stopped me from going overboard had I lost my balance.

It seems that I had been attempting a solo rendition of Leo and Kate's love scene in Titanic; unbeknownst to me - I was absolutely fast asleep. During a quiet moment the next day, I wondered if the splash of me entering the water would have woken anyone else up. I didn't count this among my near-death experiences, but it would have been a rude awakening.

The Whit Sundays and the Barrier Reef are two of the wonders of the world that I am privileged to have been able to see, not once, but twice. I would be back here with even more dramatic effect in just 12-months' time, a story you can read in *More of My Road Less Travelled…*

Back on dry land, it was safe to say I was in love with the sailing lifestyle, but we didn't have long to get our land legs back – it was time for Denmark.

Chapter 34 — Arlie Beach – The Real Parties!

Our travelling squad continued to grow; in the three days I had been floating around the Whit Sundays we had 'acquired' Katrina and Camilla, two Norwegians who would help us repel the swathes of Danes looking for a fight on game day.

Sadly, my three-day hiatus had catalysed Ayesha's lack of interest in me, and she had found an Australian surf instructor to spend time with. I was mortified on my first night back, as she glammed herself up to go out on a date with this handsome, tanned, wavy-haired, Brad Pitt body double. He was probably called Corey or Shane or something. I choose to forget. I had never met, or even seen him, but I hated the guy. I dread to think what they got up to at the lagoon.

I came up with a plan to make me feel better; there was only one thing for it. I would hit on Amy, her travelling buddy. But Tom seemed to read my mind and give me that *'don't-you-even-fucking-dare-to-think-about-it-for-even-one-second-you-devious-prick'* look so I grabbed a VB and licked my wounds trying not to think of the fun 'she who must be obeyed' was having. Oh, how I wished I was the one obeying her – my heart ached!

As it turns out, our new Norwegian friends were not anti-Danish at all. It seems not all countries hate their neighbours, and perversely, they were also much more into ski-jumping than football. But as we were in

Queensland and there was no snow to be seen, they happily painted their faces red and white and vowed to fight to the bitter end for (our) queen and our country, or something like that.

As it turned out, Denmark also donned their red and white outfits for the game, so it was hard to tell _who was whom_, especially as most of the Danes spoke better English than me. They certainly spoke better English than "Brummie Emma", who was about to make a swashbuckling entrance into our lives.

As it also turns out, the Danes were just as amicable and friendly as the Swedes had been when we played them, which, now seemed like an age ago. There would be no animosity and other than adding Scandinavian beauty and some exceptional banter, Camilla and Katrina were surplus to our nationalistic defence requirements.

It's just as well that the Danes were placid as we stuffed them 3-0, to set up a QF with the mighty Brazil. We were deeper in dreamland, even daring to believe that Baddiel and Skinner maybe, just maybe would have to change the lyrics to 'no more years of hurt'.

The Denmark team was going home but these backpacking Vikings had no intention of joining them. They shrugged off the defeat and we all danced the night away. The game a mere 90-minute separation in the shared frivolity. It was a truly wonderful atmosphere.

The parties continued in Airlie Beach. Koala's was hosting a 'foam party', which I thought would be a bit of

a naff way to ruin some of my clothes, so wasn't keen.
The rest of the gang were, however, very keen. Twenty
years before FOMO became a thing, I had FOMO, and,
was about to get foamy. My Dad would love that joke!

"First Foam at 10 p.m.," the banner soapily advertised,
which at least meant that we had the chance to drop in a
few normal bars first. Reluctantly I headed into the mess
at around 10:.30 p.m. I am glad we did. It was
debauched!

Now, I stop well short of accusing the ladies who had
taken advantage of me of rape, but I was like a lamb to
the slaughter in there. There was a bar and a 'dance floor'.
No tables, chairs or quiet booths to hang around in the
shadows; it was 'get a drink and get messy' type of place.

To limit queues at the bar it was $20 entry and then an all-
you-can-drink affair. I was handed two rum and cokes, I
was a sailor now after all, and with one drink in each hand,
I did what Sia would recommend many years later, and I
hit the dance floor. It wasn't Friday night, but I didn't
care. This foam party might turn out to be good fun after
all I mused. And it did.

One step onto the 'foam-floor' and I was immediately
engulfed, at first to the knees and then, as more bubbles
spewed from the giant pumps, to the waist. I lifted my
arms to make sure the cheap rum was not further
contaminated and, like a wounded animal raising its arms
in surrender, I was attacked by a pair of hungry Australian
girls. With my hands full, I was powerless to fight them

off and they sank their teeth into my neck. Actually, they didn't bite, rather they groped me 'appropriately' and started taking it in turns to kiss me, and then each other. I was truly helpless.

The foam provided sufficient visual protection from the rest of predators as slippery hands roamed all over me. I chugged my drinks, tossed the plastics aside (now I knew why the Aussies didn't use real glasses) and joined in the fun. The only regret was that after sharing the 'love' for a while, only one of the ladies wanted to leave for somewhere (just) a little more private.

'Sheila' the rampant Pommie-molester, dragged her prey into a taxi and back to her condo. She lived in beautiful two-bedroomed penthouse at the top of the hill. As the taxi ascended away from the backpacker zone towards more salubrious parts, I hoped that her friend who had stayed behind, would turn out to be the second resident and we could resume the menage a trois, at some point later in the night.

Before we reached the apartment, we would stop by one of the three communal pools to take a dip. We stripped naked (what, you thought we'd gone in to rinse the foam off! Come on, keep up with the story) and giggled our way into the water.

The pool lights were off; residents were supposed to vacate the water by 10 p.m., I assumed to prevent pissheads from drowning, but now I knew the real reason.

Without lights there wasn't much to see, and if anyone was watching they didn't seem to care. That was until a security guard shone a torch on us and calmly announced, "Party's over." We looked bashfully at each other as he continued, "I gave you 10 minutes, that should have been enough, and if a resident complains, it will be me up for the chop, out you get."

I had to ask for a few minutes to 'regain my composure' and let my libido subside. The guard kindly offered us a couple of towels to hide our, mainly my, embarrassment and Sheila's near perfect body. As we retired to the penthouse 'Sheels' regrettably informed me she lived alone. My hopes of a threesome dashed – for a couple more weeks at least.

The next day, it was noted by Tom that my bed had not been slept in, and he took great delight in ensuring that Ayesha was also made aware of this as the crew assembled for breakfast. Corey or Cody or Shane (?) had been a short-lived thing, but I don't think Ayesha really cared what I had been up to. In any case, I was pretty happy with the outcome. If you ever get FOMO of a foam party, you know what to do.

The foam had been a life-enhancing experience, but I was about to have a life-changing one.

A couple of nights before we were due to head on north, I would meet Emma, who was, unbeknown to me at the time, going to become a central figure in the rest of the trip, and would still be a prominent figure in my life some

20 years later, and hopefully after reading this book will remain one for the next 20+ years.

It was towards the end of one particular night out, which began as just a quiet meal and a couple of drinks. As the evening wore on, my FOMO once more aroused, Tom and I headed on to a 'music bar'*. We enjoyed the tunes for a while and even went onto the dance floor; ironically, without the foam I felt a bit naked so headed back to the bar to observe. As I propped up the bar, a beautiful young blonde lady caught my eye. As she came over, we clinked glasses and in the broadest Birmingham accent I had ever heard, she introduced herself. "Hi, I am Emma and I have a boyfriend called Steve and he's coming from Birmingham in two weeks." I quickly wracked my brain and realised I didn't know Steve from Birmingham. In fact, I didn't know anyone called Steve. I just smiled at Emma, shrugged and said, quietly into the back of my hand, "Don't worry, he's probably shagging some bird on Broad Street."** I don't think she heard me.

Emma was stunning and young, but not too young, get your minds out of the gutter for a moment please. She wasn't even as young as Ayesha.

I persuaded her to come and dance with me, and although she was pretty much completely sober, she loved it as I grinded behind her to Nelly's 'It's Getting Hot in

*Many bars specifically catered to music lovers, with loud DJ's or live bands.

**Party street in Birmingham.

Here'. Well, I say she loved it, she was laughing, so I assumed she loved it. Shortly after she would grab her bag, peck me on the cheek, say thanks for the dance and walk out the door. I was left spellbound on the edge of the dance floor. Would I ever see this stunner again?!

As it turns out, Emma was close friends with one of the new lads in Jez's dorm hut, Richard, who was also from Birmingham. The only thing thicker than his accent was his cock, which-he quite happily showed to the world any chance he got. In fact, he was naked when I met him. I wasn't quite sure which bit of his anatomy he wanted me to shake. Getting over the shock of meeting him, I then noticed Emma sitting on one of the adjacent chairs. I smiled.

That night, the group got together at Jez's hut, and we planned where to head next on our trip north. We needed to factor in where we would watch England 'kick some Brazilian Ass' and progress to the semi-final of the world cup for the first time in 12 years.

We were being pulled towards Magnetic Island ....

Chapter 35 — Magnetic Island and Mini Mokes

Magnetic Island, Maggie for short - yep, the Aussies still hadn't tired of using shortened names - was a couple of days drive north. Situated just off the coast, we aimed for a ferry in the port of Townsville. If you were on the 'Oz Bus' like most of the crew, it was a painful overnight schlep in the big green sick wagon. The freedom that Bertha gave me was incredible.

This was pretty much the first time any of us had pre-booked a hostel on the entire trip. We simply had to be together for the biggest game of football since a West German penalty left Gazza's blubbering back in 1990. We rocked up a day after the 'Oz Bus' had arrived. The atmosphere was already electric. We had two hostel rooms between us; World Cup fever was well and truly in the air.

Tom and I joined a dorm with Aysh and Amy and four of our other mates already in situ. Next door was Jez, the Norwegian girls (Camilla and Katrina), Emma, Jimmy and Naomi. They very much had the party room, which was fine by us.

We would have a couple of days to lounge around before the big game. It was to be an afternoon kick-off which meant daytime drinking and fun in the sun for us. It also meant our boys would meet Brazil in the scorching heat of Shizuoka. But for now, it was a few days to relax and let the anticipation build.

215

We hired Mini-Mokes* and explored the island. Lots of 'backpacking love' was evolving. Jimmy and Naomi were close, Ricardo and Katrina had been seen in the same bunk, Ayesha had been quiet, maybe she was waiting for me after all. I also had an eye on Emma, she was so hot, and who doesn't love a blonde, broad Brummie!

.

*Small cars that wouldn't be road worthy anywhere else in the civilised world. They looked something your five year old might drive.

Chapter 36 — Tits and Pies

For those few days it felt like the last day at school. Everyone was in a jovial mood. Endless sunny days, absolutely no agenda, everyone completely at ease with everyone else around the whole place. Everything was in flow; it was an absolutely sublime time.

Home to just 2000 or so 'real' residents, Magnetic Island is primarily a tourist spot. Palm-fringed beaches, snorkelling, walking trails and rugged forests. Bathed in 16 hours per day of Queensland sunshine 'Maggie' was the absolutely perfect location for the remainder of the World Cup. But how far would England go?

We explored the trails, ate picnics and BBQs, swam and lounged on idyllic, unoccupied beaches and the when the warm sun was replaced by warm nights, stunning stars, the moon drew us off the beaches and into the bars nearby.

I even managed to get in a round of golf, making a par on what was claimed by the Magnetic Island Country Club to be one of the 10 hardest par fours in the world (not just the southern hemisphere). Yet another outrageous Australian claim on their 'biggest and best scale', which, would no doubt be redacted by the UK's advertising standards agency if a UK club uttered such contentions. The course was beautiful but strange for a small island full of beaches, in a vast country full of beaches - there was no sand to contend with. It was the first and only course that I have played on totally devoid of bunkers.

The 'Free-Love' 1960s spirit was incredible, and our growing group was being pulled ever-closer together. I have never been so comfortable with so many people that I had hardly met, and 20 years on many of these 'backpackers' have become life-long friends.

We were an eclectic crew, from all sorts of backgrounds, but we just seemed to gel. The Norwegian girls helped to remove some of the starch from the British girls in the group and after a couple of days the transition to a completely 'laissez faire' approach to life was complete.

One morning (or early afternoon), I hopped out of my bunk, drew back the curtains to see all eight of the girls in the group lined up on sun-loungers by the pool, laid flat on their backs, every last one of them topless. I pinched myself and then smiled through the pain.

Despite Emma having the pastiest of the boobs on show, the liberation the Norwegians had given her later enabled me to sneak a quick kiss*. For some reason I was coy and respectful, we went to sleep in the fully occupied dorm room without too much fussing around. Encouraged by her words, I resolved to aim for a repeat situation the following evening.

One of the quirks of such a small island was that it was pretty self-sufficient. The majority of the residents were there to support the tourism industry. Consequently, most of the food was prepared and cooked on the island.

*For clarity, on the lips, not the boobs,

Seafood was caught fresh, fruit and veg was grown and animals reared locally. It was just far too expensive to get daily supplies over from Townsville. For me, as nice as the seafood was, it was the baked goods that I loved the most.

Bread of all varieties, from baguettes to brioche, pittas and pides, to parathas and naans, it was gluten heaven. Even better than the bread were the pies. Traditional minced meat, chicken, lamb or beef steak fillings were lovingly stuffed into freshly baked pastries of deliciousness. The Aussie bakers would also add things like hot chilli, sweet chilli, peppered cheese and other more subtle flavours to them. The options were endless and there was something sexual* about the Magnetic Island pastry. They were significantly better than the ones we had sampled in pretty much every gas station for the past 20,000 km.

Chapter 37 — Double Heartbreak – Ronaldinho and Jez

Game day. We had planned a team breakfast of bacon butties, followed by a BBQ lunch just before the game. The whole day would inevitably involve beers, but we were all quite restrained as no-one wanted to be praying to the porcelain gods while the game was on.

We, well I say 'we', it was more the girls, arranged face-painting and cobbled together England outfits; mostly consisting of white or red T-shirts and lipstick. I was a little wary of the lipstick after Melbourne. The boys talked of a possible semi-final against Turkey or Senegal.

Turkey were outsiders, dirty little scrappers, and would pull every sneaky trick in the book to win; they had very few highly talented players playing in Europe's top leagues at the time. Senegal would be a total wild card – and since Cameroon shocked the world by almost beating England in 1990, an African nation threatened to become a genuine contender every four years and we were rightly wary of the enigmatic African teams.

The consensus was that a semi-final versus Turkey would be our preferred route, but we'd be happy to play either team for what looked like being a final against our other old foe, Germany. Goodness, England does have a lot of old foes. I guess that's what being 'good' at wars does for you.

The chat about the permutations rolled on. Fuelled by those mid-morning hits of alcohol, we dared to dream the undreamable dream. We talked about semi-finals and finals, visions of Beckham hoisting the trophy aloft, and parties, serious parties, where we'd watch and how we'd celebrate.

We discussed whether we'd rather be at home with 'the country', or whether our merry band would be a better crowd. In the end we didn't care, so long as England could end almost half a century of painful exits from World Cups. Football was coming home!

Tom brought us all back to the present moment, in his inimitably pessimistic way, by reminding us we needed to beat Brazil first. "The only thing worse than not getting to the final, would be losing to the Gerries on penalties," he added, before pacing around the room, slowly walking off some of the pent-up energy. Our irreverent bubble burst.

I don't imagine that David Beckham lining up to take 'that' penalty against Argentina was anywhere close to being as nervous as Tom was that morning. Not even soothing words from Amy could calm the manic energy. The sombre focus was now the hefty task of beating Brazil. According to Tom, we were inferior in every single position. Tactically, we couldn't win and even if Brazil played their absolute worst, we still had to beat the heat. Maybe football wasn't coming home after all.

The 'glass half-fulls' among us; everyone except Tom, agreed it wasn't the strongest Brazil team to grace a World Cup. That said, in Ronaldo they had probably the best player in the world at that time. When I say probably, the debatable element of that was that Rivaldo might have been better. He was in the team too, so for this purpose it's really a moot point! They also boasted the legendary fullbacks, Cafu and Roberto Carlos who would get in most world's best teams of any era.

There was also the flamenco flair of Ronaldinho, who would twist and turn his way past his opponents and then flash them a goofy smile for good measure. For some reason, women from all over the world loved Ronaldinho, and fawned all over him; to me his smile looked more appropriate for opening my next bottle of beer. He was not liked by opposing fans.

Man for man, even an Englishman would say Brazil were favourites.

The game started well. We had all made it to the anthems without any of us being too pissed to see the screens. We were all nervous, but excited too. Jez and I gravitated to one another. Despite what Tom may have thought, Jez and I were certainly the 'most knowledgeable' ones when it came to tactics and game play (and actual play come to think of it, but that's another story).

Tom was too pessimistic to be able to see the picture of what was unfolding, so Jez and I tried to keep him quiet and shared our own nervous commentaries in the early stages. It was tense stuff. Then after 24 minutes, Michael Owen pounced on a mistake and opened the scoring. The bar erupted. I thought of my friends in the Old Country. It was as scorching hot in Queensland as it was in Japan. It was pre-breakfast and freezing cold back in Blighty.

The Brazilians looked dumbfounded as they gasped for air. "They look exhausted!" Jez gleefully noted.

I am not sure if we were more nervous or less nervous immediately after the goal. We didn't go on to dominate the game and just a few minutes later, Jez commented that Brazil were getting back into it. "It's vital we go into half-time in the lead," he mused.

Tom chimed in, "They are going to score; I can feel it."

Before we could tell him to shut the fuck up, Ronaldinho had grinned his way past four of our team and fed Rivaldo to curl an equaliser. 1-1. That was the last action of the first half. We were gutted. Naturally, we blamed Tom.

We were barely holding on at the start of the second half and it was becoming clear that our boys were tiring. It wasn't looking good.

"We need a bit of luck from a corner or a free kick, and to keep it tight at the back," grumbled Jez. We were only a couple of minutes in. It was going to be a long second half.

"We could do with a red card," added Tom, which proved to be prophetic as less than 10 minutes later, Ronaldinho was sent from the field for a potentially leg-breaking foul on Danny Mills. Sadly for us, the goofy genius had already made the score 2-1 to Brazil moments earlier.

The ref had awarded Brazil a contentious free-kick about 40 yards from goal. Roberto Carlos had looked dangerous previously, but this one was close to the touchline. David Seaman, the Arsenal keeper and England legend, authoritatively marshalled the troops and there seemed to be little danger as he patrolled his area.

We were all expecting the cross, but Ronaldinho had other ideas, sending a swirling shot over the back-peddling keeper into the top corner, leaving England stunned. Absolute silence rang through the bar, broken only by Tom, who briefly stormed off to shed a few private tears – he tried to deny he had cried when he returned shortly after with smudged face-paint. 2-1, but still another 40 minutes to get back in the game.

Trying to lighten Tom's mood, Jez quipped, "It's not the first time someone has lobbed Seaman from outside the box!" Tom was nonplussed and moaned that it could be an embarrassing scoreline if we weren't careful.

The gap-toothed wonder's red card had lifted the mood only momentarily, as England limped impotently through the remainder of the game, unable to muster the energy in the extreme heat to challenge an obdurate Brazilian team.

The game fizzled out and our dream was over.

After some more tears and a little sombre reflection, Tom unintentionally helped us get over the defeat by announcing, "Well, at least we can't lose on penalties to the fucking Gerries." Every cloud and all that!

About eight hours earlier, the same comment had struck fear into us and killed the mood but now, with that disaster having been avoided, it somehow helped lift us all. The entire crew burst into laughter. We sang the Sven-Göran Eriksson song for one last time and moved on. Football forgotten; it was time to party - again.

The day dragged on, and undeterred by England's failure to show up in the second half we pressed on. Another BBQ followed the game. We needed to soak up some of the booze or it would be an early night. Tom moped around for an hour or two, but that was not an activity solely reserved for the bitter disappointment of losing a game of football.

Jez and I continued to chew the fat about the game and as time passed, beers and burgers flowed, conversation meandered, like a summer stream, slowly through the changing landscapes of Liverpool FC, university, playing football, playing cricket, jobs and then it hit the rapids and turned to women.

Jez had split from the girlfriend shortly before coming to Australia and was asking me about my 'status'. "Nothing is going on with Ayesha, Tom loves Amy," was my initial response. I wanted to say, keep your fucking hands off Ayesha, but I just kept quiet and crossed my fingers!

He squirmed a bit, and then asked, "What about Emma?"

Having had a cheeky kiss the previous night, I was quite keen to see what she had meant by way of encouragement and a bit of fun would surely ease the pain of footballing defeat. I coyly remarked, "Her boyfriend, Super Steve, is coming out next week, it might get messy," as a half-hearted attempt to discourage him and keep my options open. Jez just grunted an acknowledgement and looked off into the distance. I went to the bar for more beers.

I am not quite sure how we all made it to the 'club' that night, but I wasn't ready to call it a night so pressed on. I was hedging on Emma or Ayesha to make my miserable soul happy, but I was about to have my heart broken for the second time in a day.

Ayesha, who was too classy to be involved in this kind if debauchery, took her leave and went off to bed. I focused on Emma, or rather I didn't, as I couldn't focus at all. I just stood nearby and swayed from side to side, somehow remaining upright. I was literally stood in the middle of the 'dance floor', unable to speak.

It felt like being in one of those dreams where you scream out for help, but no sound comes out of your mouth. I was merely an observer. Before long, Jez, somehow managing to still have the power of speech, had blown Emma's socks off with his wit and charm. I "screamed out" again in my head as they kissed. I was about two feet away – powerless. I shrugged to myself and took my broken heart off to bed. At least he hadn't kissed Ayesha!

Chapter 38 — Lifelong Mates

In the cold light of day, after a massive fry up and a swim in the freezing cold pool, I realised that I had not in fact had my heart broken. I was just pissed off that England had lost. Phew. I could move on and be happy that Emma and Jez had been sober enough to kiss away some of their pain. As things turned out, it worked out rather well for them.

That was the start of a fine romance, which is still going 20+ years later; their two lovely kids a testament to what special people they both turned into. I was a groomsman at their wedding, and I was pleased to tell the congregation that Emma is much better suited to Jez than me. I can't imagine how he has managed to put up with her for all these years! He must have the patience of a saint. Truly taking one for the team. Thanks buddy.

It was a rocky start for them. No one wants a budding relationship to begin in a dorm room, fully exposed to the eyes of the world. Those early days of exploration, and trial and error should be kept private. It was akin to falling in love in the Big Brother house!!

Despite the difficulty of discreet dorm-room fumbling, they also had the spectre of "Super Steve" arriving from Birmingham to joust for Emma's affections. It would make for an awkward week or so in Cairns after he arrived. Their plight not aided by Richard and Jimmy mercilessly ripping the piss out of Emma for dragging the guy 6000 miles to break up with him. The boys joked there should be a pugil fight to the death, with Emma as the prize!

True, the guy had travelled halfway around the world, but Jez and I had become great mates, so I wasn't going to give Steve too much sympathy. I said I would back him up if the shit hit the fan. I am glad it didn't, as I'd have been as much use as a chocolate teapot; I have never had a proper fight in my life and would probably have just gotten in the way but it's the sentiment that counts – right?

To be fair to Steve, he either was a complete legend about the whole situation, or he was secretly pleased to pass the responsibility of maintenance on to another man. Either way, he slotted nicely into the group for the short two-week trip he had booked.

It helped that Jimmy and Richard both already knew him, and that Jez was smart enough to keep a pretty low profile. During the rest of our time in Australia, Jez and I were pretty much inseparable, I think Emma even got a bit jealous at one point.

Chapter 39 — The Fire

For our final big road trip on the east coast, Jez was keener to ride with me in Bertha than on the Oz bus with Emma. As well as his love for me, it also may have had something to do with the fact that Steve was sat next to Emma on the bus.

Cairns, in far north Queensland would be the last place we would all be together - the end of the road – well the paved road at least.

Jez was riding in the back of the Bertha with Amy and Ayesha as we left Townsville on the 1-Highway. With Emma not so much front of his mind, he was trying to impress the girls! It was both comedic and cringeworthy to watch in the rear-view mirror as Tom drove us north.

No sooner had Amy and Aysh banished him from the purple love cushion, which constituted the back seat, forcing him to sit on the floor, Tom turned to me and exclaimed, "Hey, dude - we are losing power." I told him not to worry, it was probably just the incline. "We are going downhill" he retorted. I shifted uncomfortably in my chair.

Looking in the wing mirror I exclaimed, "Shit, we are on fire!"

Seemingly before we had even stopped, I jumped out to examine the engine at the rear. I didn't need to get too close as orange and blue flames licked the yellow paintwork around the air-cooler vents. Black smoke billowed. It did not look good.

"Get out!" I shouted.

Through the side window, I saw Jez clambering over Amy and Ayesha, in what I initially assumed was a bid to save himself first, but quickly realised the girls had been unable to get the dodgy sliding door open. Wide-eyed and frantic, Jez looked like an actor trying to get back into the spaceship before the doors closed and cast him in perpetuity into the abyss.

The handle on the inside was stuck, again. One of the many things we were due to fix in Cairns. Fortunately, just like Superman, Tom appeared from nowhere and slid the door open.

Jez fell through the open gap and onto the hard shoulder. He looked at the flames and then at me and asked, "Do you think we should get the bags out?"

Our backpacks were stacked on the shelf at the back of the van, just above the flames. Before I could respond, he started to run down the road like he was escaping from a dragon from Game of Thrones.

Superman then swept the two distressed damsels into his arms and carried them to safety. Well, that's how Tom tells it. Ayesha later explained she had to kick him in the balls so she could get through the door as he was "faffing over Amy" – which is a much more believable story. Either way, we were all safe and congregated some 30 metres up the road. The fire was well and truly taking hold.

I looked around. After what seemed like an eternity, Jez re-asked his question, "Should we go back for the backpacks?" Before anyone had chance to reply, there was an almighty explosion and amidst a huge fireball the side door was blown clean off and ended up halfway down the embankment. Michael Caine would have been proud.

We looked at Bertha, bubbling like an erupting volcano, and then at each other. I was wearing only board shorts. No thongs, not even a wife beater. I checked my head, relieved that my 'real' Oakley's which I had almost lost during that Thai beach massage nine months prior, were still on my head. I put them on to shield my eyes from the fire.

The five of us stood there in the middle of the road. There were no cars to worry about as they were all stationary, watching on like extras in a film. All we could see was a huge traffic jam. Both directions were at a complete standstill. The queues growing longer and longer. We had blocked the only main road north from Townsville. Horns honked so loud it felt like they were inside my head.

Then all of a sudden, Jez's phone rang. A stroke of luck that it was in his pocket. It was Rob. "Dude, we are in a traffic jam on the 1-Highway, avoid it if you can, it looks like a car is on fire in front."

"We can't avoid it buddy," Jez replied. "It's us. Bertha's going up in flames."

Before Jez could reassure Rob that we were all alive and well, he and a couple of the others came sprinting up the road to see for themselves. Between the five of us we had one wallet, one phone, three pairs of thongs and two wife beaters. Just about enough clothes between us to not be arrested if we walked through a shopping mall.

By the time the fire brigade arrived, some 90 minutes later, all that was left of Bertha was four tyres melted into the road and a mess of mangled metal which had been the chassis; and of course, the side door, smouldering away on the embankment.

The heat had been so extreme that the road surface had sunk about 18 inches. It looked like the van was digging its own grave and being cremated at the same time.

Chapter 40 — The Aftermath

There's nothing like a near-death experience to focus your mind on the things you want most in life. I focused on Ayesha.

But first we needed to start to sort this mess out! "Where are we?" I asked the fireman.

"Rolling Stone," came the reply. I just nodded.

Population: 43, Rolling Stone was, how should I put it? Sleepy. The fireman was called Bruce.-I know, they all seem to be called Bruce – what do you want me to do about it? Make the names up? He was also the policeman and the local baker. He had clearly been focused on preventing his pies from burning, rather than saving Bertha.

Actually, he was lovely and explained that the local fire brigade has one truck for a gazillion square fathoms of bush, or some similar ratio, and they'd been on call 'just up the road' at the next town (population 76), a mere 100 km away. Presumably it was called "Gathers No Moss".

The big-rig, as he called it, had made it from Townsville nearly as fast as the local one made it back from the next town. Either way, Bertha was reduced to dust long before they arrived and hardly a hose had been squirted in anger. I mention the big-rig, not because it played any functional role on the day, but because it was the cause of a series of letters to me, from the Queensland Fire Service.

They wrote to me about six times over the following year, politely requesting that I pay the $300 call out charge for their fire truck's attendance at the fire. Now, I am not averse to using an outcall service, but I wouldn't pay for it if the main event was already over! So, I politely ignored the first five letters. Finally, I wrote them a letter by reply.

Dear QFS,

I will not be paying a charge for the call out of the fire truck.

I realise that Australia is a big country, but you took so long to show up to the fire that my OTL (one true love) Bertha was reduced to a pile of dust. There was barely even a flame by the time you arrived and a kangaroo taking a piss could have put out the fire just as efficiently as you did.

The fire left me with absolutely nothing. No passport, no money, no clothes and no photos of your beautiful country. All that I have left are my sweet memories which are fast being tainted by this callous pursuit.

Furthermore, my phone also did not survive so it couldn't have been me that called out the truck. So, I suggest that you take this up with the busybody who dialled the emergency number.

Yours sincerely,
Andrew Shaw

PS. I am still in mourning over Bertha so
please respect my privacy at this time.

I did not hear from them again.

I was glad to find on my return to the country just under two years later that I was not arrested for the unpaid bill. I was fortunate to be entering in a different state, so either their systems didn't talk to each other, or they just didn't hold a grudge.

As I passed through the 'nothing to declare' sign at the airport, I decided that the $300 stashed in my wallet, just in case I was shown into a customs room on entry, could now be reappropriated towards a bottle of bubbly and a celebration.

Before I get ahead of myself, I have to make it around the rest of world before I can tell you about my return to Oz.

After we had made our statements at Rolling Stone Police Station, we hitched a lift back to Townsville, the shithole of a place we had escaped that same morning. It was now dark so it didn't look quite as bad. We borrowed money from Rob and got our heads down for the night at the hostel. You know, the one with the dodgy lift. I looked around for Punxsutawney Phil. It was literally Groundhog Day for us.

Losing your passport and wallet abroad is a challenge. At least I spoke the local language, or more accurately I could just about make myself understood. Despite being repeatedly told that it was impossible to apply for a new passport from Australia by the UK embassy in Canberra, I finally managed to make them see sense and get me a replacement sent out. It would take 7-10 days. I had it sent to Cairns. No fucking way was I hanging around in Townsville for more than a week!

Money was an even bigger problem. My bank (after this trip, ex-bank) just laughed at me when I told them to send me a replacement ATM card to Australia, so it was down to my dad to send money by Western Union money transfer.

A couple of days earlier I had called him and said, "Hi Dad, don't worry, I am absolutely fine, but the van blew up and burned to a cinder along with everything I own." When I called him again for help with money, he was happy to oblige.

The first time he tried to send me cash he had dashed into town before work, but was unable to complete the Western Union form. He was told that the receiver of the funds must be able to produce appropriate ID to the shop owner in order for them to release the money. I had no passport, driving licence and, "The dirty-looking blonde guy in black and green Boardies and no T-shirt" apparently wasn't robust enough.

Big Al (my dad) put his thinking cap on overnight and went back to WU and filled in the forms. He persuaded the money man, and my funds were on the way.

When I turned up the next day to collect my money, the vendor took my name and looked at his screen. He looked up at me and said, "Take your shirt off." I paused, not expecting to have to offer 'services' for my money. The look of horror in my eyes was spotted by the vendor who quickly added, "You need to show your tattoos as verification of who you are."

Relieved, I flashed my bronzed six-pack and inked deltoids (ok, the six-pack was more of a barrel). He handed me an envelope.

With a fist full of dollars, I was set. First purchase, a beer! Well, solvency was worth celebrating, right? As Jez and I sipped our beers, I mused, *"Huh, I didn't know my dad knew about my tatts"*.

I called him later and after I'd thanked him for the umpteenth time, he said, "Don't tell your mother about the way you ID'd yourself, she still doesn't know about the ink!"

My second purchase was a wallet, the third was a train ticket north for the following day. Hopefully Ayesha would still be there.

The next day was fun. Before the train left at 2:15 p.m., we went to a few shops to buy essentials, including three pairs of boxers, I had had enough of going commando, my own T-shirt (I wasn't having any more of that wife beater shit either) and some new thongs. Oh, and a bag to carry them in. Jez suggested we stopped for lunch. I checked the time with a passer-by and worked out we had 45 minutes to spare.

Over a sandwich and a Coke, we pondered the past few days and then journey ahead. We mainly focussed on how hard we would celebrate being alive when we got to Cairns. This really had been a near-death experience.

At just before 2 p.m. we sauntered towards the station, thinking we had 15 mins before our train was due to leave; we were urged to hurry by staff in the foyer. They were waving arms and shouting at us to run. We legged it across the bridge, down the stairs. Now running hard, we leapt, like panting dogs through the beeping doors just moments before they closed behind us with a hydraulic whoosh.

Giggling, I looked at Jez lying prone next to me and laughed, "Made it."

"Just," he snorted.

A gruff Aussie voice drew our eyes upwards as we were confronted by the train guard. Thinking we were about to get a telling off, he sternly looked at his watch and announced, "Good job you did make it, the next train north is in three days from now."! I had miscalculated the time! Next item to buy was a watch – but not one of those Balinese specials!

We had eight hours to ponder the fact that trains between two (real sized) towns only run once every three days. I reflected how lucky we were to get a fire truck in just 90 minutes. I wondered what the train driver did on non-train days. Maybe he was a part-time fireman. We passed the time snoozing and filling in our insurance claims. When you make a list like that you realise how much stuff you can get in a 30l pack.

Chapter 41 — The Crowning Glory

Cairns is the most northerly City on the east Coast of Australia. It's a party place. Aren't they all?!

When not partying, the locals making their livings from fishing and tourism. Cairns has easy access to the Great Barrier Reef, the Daintree Rain Forest and the eco-tourism destination of Cape Tribulation, but above all I loved the fact that it has a suburb called Yorkeys Knob. Don't roll your eyes at me! You got this far and there's not long to go now.

Northern Queensland really is a naturalists'* dream with wildlife, beautiful landscapes and sublime sunrises and sunsets. If only I had a campervan to roam around in.

I eventually got to see some of the nature on offer, spotting 10-metre long and 10cm long crocodiles in the same river, kangaroos, tree snakes and the biggest spider I have ever seen. Sadly, still no koala in the wild.

Initially Jez and I weren't too worried about the wildlife and going on treks. Jez's mind was on Emma and sneaking the odd snog without rubbing Super Steve's nose in it. Also on his mind was the fact he had a flight to Thailand in less than two weeks and as yet, no replacement passport.

*Naturalist or Naturist, I am never totally sure which is which. There was a lot of nature to look at, is my point!

After our daily check for deliveries at the local post office, we spent our time lounging round the pool re-united with all the guys from Magnetic Island. Evenings ended up in the Woolshed.

Tom, Ayesha and Amy had already made it to Cairns safely and the five of us needed to buy some more essentials. Thongs, Boardies and a selection of Queensland wife beaters. Although personally I was back to T-shirts, the others favoured vests, especially the ones sporting Castlemaine XXXX branding*. We were nothing if not predictable.

We enjoyed mooching around and generally just celebrating being alive after coming within a few seconds of being blown down the embankment with the van door.

Jez's passport eventually arrived. Just two days before his flight. Everyone except Tom and I were about to leave Australia. Tom was headed back to Adelaide to teach more kids tennis and I had some time to kill before being joined by two mates from the UK.

Jez, Emma, Rob, Amy and Ayesha were heading to Thailand. Several of the group, including Steve, heading back home to the UK the very next day. The mood was a bit melancholy, especially among those heading home, but we were all determined to have one last cracking night out to celebrate our time together.

The Woolshed is still going in 2021 (at time of

Yeah, another beer!

publishing) and is presumably still called the "Pullshed" by all who frequent it. It's a bit of a dive but the cheap liquor brings in the backpackers and locals in their droves - every night of the week. We all donned our glad rags for one final hurrah. I looked like (slightly lumpy) model from a Quicksilver catalogue in my new threads.

And, whilst this story has been largely a tale of funnies, failures and fuck-ups, that last night together gave me the epic Hollywood love story ending I was hoping for!

After a lot of group chatting, hugging and promises of staying in touch after our travels, we all ended up on the dance floor, Ayesha came over to me, and midway through our first dance together, she gently pulled my head down and whispered in my ear, "Are you ever going to kiss me? If you don't do it now, it will be too late."

Epilogue —Twelve Pints of Kilkenny

After a semi-tearful goodbye, the "East Coast" group had disbanded. Dave and Danny, who shall henceforth be knowns as Dan (for reasons to be explained) had arrived from the UK on a month-long hiatus from their corporate jobs.

Dan is a spy – I can't tell you what he actually does, or I may have to kill you, if he didn't kill me first. Dave works for the Devil, he teaches kids.

We were three English lads, best friends from uni, re-united with a lot to catch up on. What could be more natural than to get started in a dingy corner of a bog-standard Irish bar, which are ubiquitous worldwide. We may as well have been back in Loughborough.

Both the boys were thoroughly jetlagged, and *'I had been travelling about nine months (!).'** so it wasn't unnatural for us to be in the pub just before noon. "Three Kilkennys" was the order, which would be repeated a dozen or so times over the course of the next 10 hours.

Their flight from Heathrow, via LA had been eventful and they had enjoyed little sleep, partly because the third occupant on their row was a larger-than-life, in more ways than one, American who had snored and dribbled all the

---

An inside joke cracked shortly after we almost slid to our deaths on a New Zealand glacier (yes, you can read about it in my next book).

way across the Atlantic Ocean.

Unable to sleep with Fatty hanging over the side of the chair, Dave, just a few hours into his month of relaxation, sought retribution and blasted out the loudest, smelliest fart imaginable*, much to the disgust of his confederate friend next door, who had been ingloriously ripped from his slumber.

Much to Dan's amusement, Dave immediately shut his eyes, pretending to sleep and trying not to burst into laughter. The two of them had spent the subsequent seven hours trying not to make eye contact with anyone else on the plane.

This was pretty much the limit of their funny stories from the previous month, but I was happy to regale them with some of my anecdotes. About nine or ten beers in, just when I thought I was done, Dave remembered an email I had sent him a few short weeks ago.

"Tell us what happened with the pies on that island."

With my fear of embarrassment washed away by the Kilkenny, I inhaled and began.

"Ah, you mean Magnetic Island?" I enthused. "Well, I was explaining to two of the girls, that I had found a bakery in the middle of nowhere. It was three in the morning and I had got myself not one but two freshly baked pies to keep me satiated for walk home.

Dave is world renowned for both volume and pungency.

"And as you guys know, I have been known to make the odd outrageous claim in my time, so naturally they didn't believe me." The boys laughed and jibed that even if it was true, it was a shit story, but I would have the last laugh.

"Hang on," I said holding my hand up like a traffic cop, slightly slurring my words, "There's more."

The girls argued it wasn't possible and I was just taking them for a ride. I imitated a girl's voice and bobbed my head incredulously, "Even if you did find a bakery, there's no way they'd serve you at 3 a.m." Dan and Dave laughed along.

I was pretty sure that I hadn't made it up, and as my mind flashed back to the kebab shop in Bondi, so I said I would prove it to them.

One of the girls, so disbelieving, responded, "I will have sex with you on the beach if we can get pies after 1 a.m.".

""Me too", the other chimed in.

""Threesome?" I laughed.

"They looked at each other and nodded. "You're on!" they chimed in unison.

"I couldn't wait for the end of the night. We left the pub at just after 1 a.m. in search of beef and onion, corned beef and chicken curry pies. I estimated that we were no more than ten minutes away from the bakery.

"Fifteen minutes later, we were wandering around the barely-lit suburban streets where I had remembered the bakery to be. It was nowhere to be seen. It was like Bondi all over again but this time the stakes were higher.

We turned left and right, all the small streets looked the same and somehow we seemed to have doubled back and saw the same house again."

Dan and Dave were now transfixed, in disbelief, or maybe it was the beers and the jetlag, or maybe just my shite story telling. But I continued, "I was hungry for pie, in more ways than one, but getting a little despondent. I think the girls were just hungry! Every turn, my dreams were dashed. My luck must have run out in Bondi I mused.

"It was time to give up and admit that I had indeed had the most lucid dream of my entire life. How cruel the dream gods can be."

"Losing patience, the girls started to head for the hostel. Defeated and deflated, I wandered some 20 yards behind in quiet contemplation. All I could think was how embarrassing the whole thing was and how I hoped that there were some crisps in the hostel vending machine…"

"Just then, the girls burst out laughing, hands covered mouths and then a squeal. Slowly, fingers were pointed and then a louder scream. They turned to me yelling, "It's there, it's there!" as they jumped up and down for joy. We headed for the bakery door.

"I got there moments after the girls, but their jollity was abruptly halted by the 'Closed' sign. Reviewing the 'opening hours' which clearly stated that 4 p.m. was the closing time not 4 a.m. as I had suggested.

"They faux bitch-slapped me and called me a tease. I reaffirmed, "So, if we all get pies, we go eat them on the beach and have a threesome?

""Yes, but it's closed, dickhead," one of them said. "You are so full of shit, you couldn't even handle one of us, let alone both," they teased.

"Aiming to save face, I knocked on the door and a light came on in the shop. The guy came to the door and mouthed "W-E A-R-E C-L-O-S-E-D" and pointed to the sign.

""Get the chef," I mouthed back, "he served me last night." The guy went away, and the light went off. A couple of minutes passed, and no-one came so I knocked again, motivated into action by the girls' threats to leave.

"The light came on again and a different face approached the door. He turned the lock and opened the door ajar. As he peeked through the small gap, the light from the window display lit up my face and he looked shocked.

""Haha, you again, and you brought hot friends!"

"We stepped inside, and he turned the main light off and locked the door. "You'd better be quick and choose what you want!" I knew exactly what I wanted and five minutes later, we were on the beach jollity resumed."

Dave cut in, "Great story, but you can't half drag out a yarn, Mr Shaw... I am gonna puke if we don't get some air." So, 12 pints of Kilkenny in, we left O'Blarnies and wobbled our way back to the hostel.

We had an early start the next day and in what seemed like no time at all, we were rudely awoken by three simultaneous alarms. We had a bus to catch.

Greener than a Greenpeace activist in a green t-shirt at a rally in Greenland, Dave and Dan emerged about three minutes before the bus was due. I was relatively bright-eyed and had even managed to pick up some snacks and fruit for the journey.

We waited outside wondering if we'd missed the bus or maybe we were in wrong place for the pick-up. The big bus lurched into view. The sickly green colour of the bus matched that of Dan's cheeks.

We took our seats right in the middle of the 50-seater and looked around at the poor bastards who had our company for (at least) that day.

Trying to make conversation, Dave returned to the previous night. "So, Shaw, what happened on the beach?"

Before I got a chance to answer, Dan, interjected. "Can we just be quiet, lads, I feel like I might puke at any moment, and Mr Shaw, *please,* no more Australia stories…This is New Zealand….

To be continued…

ABOUT THE AUTHOR

Who am I? That's a good question…I will let you know
as soon as I have found out.

If you want some labels, I am a father, friend, son,
entrepreneur, sport lover, contrarian thinker, speaker,
coach, business owner and self-crowned comedian – If
the book does well, I will keep that label.

I am me. Trying, day by day, to show up as the best
version I can; and going to sleep better for the
experience. Maximising every minute of life.
Imperfectly perfect, vulnerable, living and speaking my
truth about the things that matter to me.

My time spent travelling the world in 2002 was me
living my best life as a 24-year-old. Somewhere
between then and starting to write this book I got lost.
The book marks my return to living my best life now
and there's much more to come from me.

Find out more at www.AndrewShaw.blog
Follow me on social:
Instagram @andrewshaw.blog
Facebook @AndrewShaw.blog

ANDREW SHAW

AndrewShaw.blog

Keep an eye out for the follow up to this book
"More of a Road Less Travelled"
and if you buy that, I will write the final part of the
trilogy!

For more information about our books, or to submit a manuscript, please visit

www.green-cat.shop